THE POWER
OF I WILL

It *WILL* Change Your Life

~ Josh ~
To live by Faith &
honor our God   Heb 11:13

In Christ

The Power of I Will

For information about this title or to order other books and/or electronic media, contact the publisher:

Pilgrim-Way

www.journey-man.org

ISBN: 978-0-9832306-0-1 paperback
       978-0-9832306-1-8 ebook

Cover and interior design: 1106 Design

Illustrations: Dore Bible Illustrations, *www.creationism.org/images/*

All scripture was taken from the New International Version Bible.

ULTIMATE POWER

THE POWER OF I WILL

It *WILL* Change Your Life

C.W. EDDY

Dedication

To my dear wife, Angela, who believes in me.

To Dr. Ron Cottle, who is a fantastic scholar and Bible teacher.
Each topic seems to be his favorite!

To the seeker . . . may we meet and worship together.

Table of Contents

Author's note

It has been my intent to make this book an example of simplistic persuasion. I have tried to resist the temptation to compete on some levels with a world of "bells and whistles." You will notice several illustrations in this book. They were included and left in their black and white format—simplistic and yet making a statement. Many people are visual learners . . . a picture can evoke an emotion or conclusion as much or more than words. Some of my anecdotes have a Western cultural flavor that could be lost to your frame of reference. It is my belief that this book may be viewed by those who cannot fully understand the verbiage and maybe even by some who cannot read; that the message of this book may be conveyed and shared by some who might even have to hide its meaning from those who would censure it. Those who would desire "ultimate power" can often be the ones most afraid of "the power of I will."

"What's up with the geese?"

*T*he word migrate can mean to move, either permanently or seasonally, from one place to another. You and I are on a migration. Whether of our own will or the call of nature, we are being called "homeward." May this book be the key in the freedom to follow that call!

"Great truths and true friends are much alike—if you find even a few, and they last through life—you are blessed."

—C. W. Eddy

Introduction

Excuse me. Yeah . . . excuse me. May I have your attention?

That's a good way, I suppose, to get somebody's attention. . . . I mean, you weren't looking for me. However you stumbled upon this book, I know I only have a few seconds to hook you. By the way . . . were you looking for a self-help book? Maybe you were interested in a book on willpower? Or maybe you're sick of that whole popular genre.

The self-help genre really isn't anything new though. It's just that we have learned how to market the daylights out of most anything these days. You can go to the supermarket or bookstore and find just about any number of books on self-improvement.

I must be honest, I am greatly interested in your and my own self-improvement. But, frankly, I don't really care if you lose those few extra pounds, or make that final breakthrough at work, or in the boardroom, or in the bedroom . . . While those all may be good, I think there is an even deeper reality to this life we live.—DUH?—Hey, I heard that.

WELL . . . ISN'T THERE?

"Honey—You can be *anything* you want to be," says Mommy.

"Be all that you can be," says the Army.

"Whatever will be, will be," says the World.

These common thoughts, which are practically programmed into us, are meant to be good advice as we walk through the journey of life. I am not about to comment much on any of them; one is meant to comfort and inspire, another to challenge, and yet another to accept the things you cannot change. There are many, many resources to back up any of these sayings. Books and web sites abound with a great deal of well-intended and well-thought-out guidance for doing great things in life. I will not for one minute make light of the phenomenal accomplishments that humans have done under the most arduous conditions. I, personally, do not believe that you can become anything you want. Maybe I'm too much the pragmatist, but by all means, I want us to become what we were intended to be!

So with the above disclaimers, so to speak, in place, and without famous quotes to cloud the mix, let us begin.

"Excuse me—can I have your attention?"

I want you to know from the very beginning I plan to treat you with respect. I am honored that you have chosen to walk with me. What do I mean by that? Just this: our time together is like a walk. You will allow me to talk with you for the next several days. I do hope you don't prove to me how fast you can read! That would be a little like the teenager who has to be coaxed to the dinner table, and instead of enjoying the hard work and loving intent of the hands that prepared the meal, engulfs it and bolts! Probably to do something really important, . . . like texting a friend . . . to like . . . tell them they are breathing. "Whatever!" I say that tongue in cheek, because some of you may be parents and know what I mean. But the point is, reader: I have labored to put together a fresh and, hopefully, enlightening, work here. It is purposely short so that you might not be overwhelmed, but chew on each chapter and each thought. It may have some answers you were searching for. You may have **no idea** how much power there is in just two little words! I guarantee that you will not get through life without drawing your own conclusion regarding the issues I will bring forth.

I want you to take this book at a comfortable pace. I prepared it especially for you. You might be surprised at some of the "entrees in this meal." Do any of the following topics interest you? World Religions, Willpower, Virgin Birth, Creation and Evolution, Conception, Free Will, Grace versus Legalism, True Love, and much more? I want you to think and use the questions at the end of each chapter as a springboard to your growth. Please write notes in the margins and do some library or Internet searches of your own.

If you are reading these words I know that you have *willpower*, *will*, and *power*. I acknowledge and respect that in humankind. I also think there is a cumulative or collective will of people. Have you ever noticed how a huge flock of birds can abruptly change course in midair before settling on a wire or landing in a field? I wonder in what ways that we, as societies or people groups, exhibit similar patterns of behavior? But for the sake of this book, we will concentrate on each of us as individuals. For that matter, you personally: for since the inception of this book, I have asked designers and editor alike, "What did it do for you? What did you personally take away from our time together?"

Throughout this book I will do my very best to keep to a central theme. I will try to keep things as simple as my brain can compile them. I intend to suggest that there is a great deal we can learn in regard to THE WILL, in regard to POWER, and specifically, consequences.

> WILL . . . (noun): **1.** The power of conscious, deliberate action: the faculty by which the rational mind makes choice of its ends of action and directs the energies in carrying out its various determinations: in popular usage, choice, purpose or directive effort.

> POWER . . . (noun): **1.** Ability to act: potency, specifically, the property of a substance or being that is manifested in effort or action, and by virtue of that substance or being, produces change, moral or physical. **2.** Potential capacity.

Please read the above words once more. They are key to unlocking some of life's great mysteries!

I think I can safely say that in the pages to follow I will convince you that this is not another self-help book. It is my hope that I will get you to consider, rather just than step on toes, some issues and viewpoints that may be new to you. How we view, and act, in this exercise we call life *can and does* have eternal consequences.

It is my hope that this book will find its way into the hands of a wide variety of people. From soldiers stationed away from home, to students across the world, to the religious community as well as seekers, skeptics and scholars. I have kept it to a certain length on purpose. I want it to be used by study groups and enjoyed by those who may not want to tackle a thick work on one certain topic. Rather than enlarge it for the sake of market pressure, I took the advice of another wise storyteller, who oftentimes ended a riveting dialogue with, "that's all I have to say about that." (Forrest Gump)

THE CREATION OF LIGHT
And the earth was without form, and void.   Genesis 1:2-3

For discussion sake, what is the artist trying to portray in this picture?

What might be right (–or wrong–) with this portrayal?

What is light?

Chapter 1

In the Beginning:
a very good place to start

*O*h, by the way, I will be talking about
God quite a lot in this book. Well, I told you it was not a typical self-help book. In fact He was there in the beginning. You see—there was a beginning. Even something as simple as that can make a whole lot of folks uncomfortable. No kidding! You see, some people just don't like to think that simply. If you put *the beginning* back far enough, like maybe thousands of years. "Excuse me! Impossible!" Okay, then millions of years. "AHH-hem! Still a little uncomfortable here!" Okay; well, billions of years ago, there was a beginning.

I read a book once. It has been the world's best seller for longer than I can remember. In fact, it was a best seller before there ever was a Wal-Mart or self-help books, maybe even before there were bookshelves! It says, "In the beginning God." I am not trying to be a wise guy. We are on a course of considering will—and power. We need to lay some groundwork.

The word Genesis means "beginning." If something had a beginning, if it is here now, it had to be created. We cannot, or should not, avoid seriously examining evolution or creation. Some believe that upon the choice between the two hinges the very foundations of one's worldview. And please know that everyone has a worldview, whether the graduate student or the gravedigger, the "egghead" to the "crackhead." I also must say that it is sad to me that some are so bound by addictions, abuse, or maybe just their hectic schedules that they cannot look much past surviving to even consider some very important issues.

1. What is the fundamental issue concerning the acceptance of creation or evolution?
   a. Origins. Where did we come from?
   b. Will you accept a natural or supernatural reason for your existence?
   c. Acceptance of creation or evolution is foundational to all our thinking.
   d. The acceptance of creation or evolution determines our worldview.
   e. All thinking is either going to be done in obedience to God or in disobedience to God.

If you are an evolutionist I mean no disrespect by what I am about to say. I just don't have enough "faith" to believe in that system for explaining the world I live in. We both have to admit that we were not there for the beginning of this drama, whether that beginning was billions or thousands of years ago. We must also agree that science is a body of knowledge, where each fact is, or should be, observable, measurable, repeatable, and predictable. This is, at least, how it should be. But our beliefs are not always based on facts and evidence. And from these two facts we form a hypothesis. Some scientists' findings, if we really look at them, are nothing more than beliefs and hypotheses. If we are truly honest we will have to admit that evolution is like this: it's just a belief and not an established fact. A belief can be based on fact, or preponderance of evidence, or completely on bias. Isn't it utterly amazing that we humans sometimes hold on to beliefs far more dearly than science? We will develop this thing called believing more in later chapters.

Given that both positions; creation or evolution, are beliefs and that they must be taken largely by faith, I will not try to have a "smackdown" and beat the reader into submission with an overload of data and argument. I do however, believe that there are terrific apologetic facts and arguments that any serious believer should be aware of and use in spreading the 'Good News'. But I don't believe that to be a Christian or person of faith that one must turn off their intellect as they accept things by faith. On the contrary! The God I believe in is so majestic and powerful—and **personal**—that He delights in tailoring some of these proofs to the specific way we are "wired." By that I mean that if someone is fascinated by astronomy, there are wonders to be discovered that point to His intelligent design and plan. . . . If one is amazed at language—He is the master communicator . . . if it's art—He is the author of color, light, and hue . . . and so on.

Throughout this book I will try to make us think by giving my opinion. I will admit my bias and lean on what God says in His word as authoritative and inspired. It can be a little unnerving to hold onto a position that you can be challenged or confronted on. It is also not easy to come to grips with something that is foreign to what has been taught as fact during our formative years; that can lie subliminally, if not overtly, in cartoons, television, documentaries, movies, and magazines that constantly confront us.

I respect the educated and do not try to be the rebel, but, I will never forget learning that over 500 people did their doctoral dissertations on Piltdown Man. In case you never heard of him let me acquaint you two. Piltdown Man was one of the most famous frauds in the history of science. In 1912 Charles Dawson discovered the first of two skulls found in the Piltdown quarry in Sussex, England. Skulls were found of an apparently primitive hominid, an ancestor of man. Piltdown Man, or *Eoanthropus Dawsoni,* to use his scientific name, was a sensation. He was the expected "missing link," a mixture of human and ape with the noble brow of *Homo sapiens* and the jawbone of an ape.

In 1953 you might not have wanted to admit you used that finding to prop up your evolutionary position. The hoax was exposed. The "missing link" was a combination of medieval skull, elephant molar, hippo and canine teeth. The ingredients of this "ancestor" were gathered from different places and underwent special treatments to make them appear ancient.

One thing about the above story is that it tells us a little about education and science. The scientist is biased. He is not totally objective. He is human and consequently fallible. But he can influence a great many people!

The evolutionary approach as to our origins uses a formula that may look something like this:

1. Eternal Matter + Eternal Energy + Eternal Time + Random Chance = Life.
   a. Randomness and chaos.
   b. Long periods of time.

The creation approach as to our origins uses a formula like this:

2. Matter + Energy + Intelligence = Life.
   a. Designer, Creator.
   b. Purpose and meaning.

Will you participate in a little mental exercise here with me now? I would ask you in the space following to scribble down a little formula of your own. How would you put in formula form or equation, your view of life or where you are now in time and space?

I, as you may have guessed, believe in creation. In fact I believe in "abrupt appearance" rather than "gradual appearance" in how things came into being. This may date me a little, but when I think of abrupt, I think of a couple of word pictures or phrases. One is John Madden. Do you remember him? He was the popular sports announcer and a voice for many things from football—to—foot care! When John talked about a running back hitting a gap to make a spectacular play it was always "BOOM" and he got through, or "BOOM" and the foot fungus was relieved! Another saying I think of when thinking about something happening suddenly is "in a New York minute." I think that kind of means, RIGHT NOW—with an ATTITUDE!

I admit I believe in the Bible. I believe in Genesis. I even believe there was an actual beginning set of people we can call Adam and Eve. I don't have enough faith to believe that the absolutely awesome unit called human being evolved from primordial ooze. And I don't believe that Adam waited around a few thousand years for his female counterpart unit, i.e. Eve, to show up on the scene. So here we are . . . you and me . . . we get to go back in time, to the time of Adam and Eve. You and I are hiding behind a boulder or something when all of a sudden in "A NEW YORK MINUTE!" there appears Adam. "Wow! Did you see that?" I mean come on, if he existed, he had a physical appearance. Did he start out as a toddler? I think "BOOM" here he is, maybe thirty years old or the appearance thereof. So, if I can be crazy enough to believe in an account like this, it is not a stretch for me to believe God can instantly create something out of nothing. That is called *Creatio Ex Nihilo* just to throw a little Latin in there to impress ya! That means that out of nothing God created space, time and matter. He spoke it into existence. He didn't make it out of pre-existing elements such as earth, wind, fire, water, like many religions believe.

Your opinion matters.

What is the artist trying to suggest here?

What period of world history has art you most like?

So come with me back to the Garden of Eden where we saw Adam. He looks like a man . . . Has some age—instantly created but has the beginnings of a five o'clock shadow! You get my point? By the way, did I mention that behind that boulder we happened to bring along a chain saw? Oh yeah! And you know boys with chain saws? We want to cut something down! So we take out a tree because there are plenty of them anyway. Guess what? It has growth rings that show up in the stump. Humph! Something created yet with the appearance and suggestion of age!

I forgot to mention that we also have a big ol' gun with us behind that boulder. Well, as our story goes, it is getting along in the day and we was getting hungry. You know, we was out looking for some food, so we shot at sumthin' . . . and out from the ground came "a bubblin' crude". . . . Oil that is! There I go dating myself again. I make light of the old Beverly Hillbillies song to make a point. Oil. Something that science tells us only forms over millions of years under specific circumstances and earth periods.

One of my favorite things to do, when I can afford it, is to go scuba diving. I have had the privilege of going to some remarkable locations and enjoying God's creation. I am amazed that He would create such a vast and diverse environment even though it was not able to be interfaced with nor captured on film until relatively recent history as far as the age of mankind is concerned. I marveled as I personally watched large predatory fish come to an area known as a "cleaning station." These fish come with the accumulated parasites and debris in their mouths from eating other fish and sea creatures. They come to the station, open their mouths and allow specific species of cleaner fish and shrimp to do their jobs. What prevents them from clamping down with those dangerous teeth and making a meal of their servants? What causes those servants to know that this is a safe zone, whereas they may be lunch any other time and any other place than this for those same predators? Evolutionists claim that trial and error, time and random chance can explain something like this. Sometimes, after witnessing such amazing sights, I have just raised my hands in praise—weightless—while doing my safety stop below the surface. This last sentence in itself reminds me of what the Bible tells us.

> *For since the creation of the world, God's invisible qualities—his eternal power and divine nature—have been clearly seen, being understood from what **has been made,** so that men are without excuse. For although they knew God, they neither glorified him as God nor gave thanks to him, for their thinking became futile and their foolish hearts became darkened.*
> —Romans 1:20-21 *(my emphasis)*

I told you that I am biased . . . that humans are biased . . . that we formulate our worldview on a vast montage of information and prejudice. While this chapter is not trying to force feed a creationist perspective, let me leave that topic with a thought on one more marvel, some of which is easily found in a simple Internet search, and some that comes from courses I have studied.

The Human Eye
Evolutionists are hard-pressed to explain the step-by-step accidental development of the human eye, which is characterized by a staggering complexity. Furnished with automatic aiming, automatic focusing, and automatic aperture adjustment, the

human eye can function from almost complete darkness to bright sunlight, see an object the diameter of a fine hair, and make about 100,000 separate motions in an average day, faithfully affording us a continuous series of color stereoscopic pictures. All of this is performed usually without complaint, and then while we sleep, it carries on its own maintenance work.

The human eye is so complex and sophisticated that scientists still do not fully understand how it functions. Considering the absolutely amazing, highly sophisticated synchronization of complex structures and mechanisms that work together to produce human vision, it is difficult to understand how evolutionists can honestly believe that the eye came about through a step-by-step trial and error evolutionary process. This is especially true when we realize that the eye would be useless unless fully developed. It either functions as an integrated whole or not at all. Clearly, the piecemeal evolution of the human eye is a completely outlandish and unreasonable notion.

Even Charles Darwin acknowledged how one might have difficulty in accepting the concept of developing an eye through mutation and natural selection. The following quotation comes from Darwin himself.

> *To suppose that the eye, with all its inimitable contrivances for adjusting the focus to different distances, for admitting different amounts of light, and for the correction of spherical and chromatic aberration, could have been formed by natural election, seems, I freely confess, absurd in the highest possible degree. . . . The belief that an organ as perfect as the eye could have formed by natural selection is more than enough to stagger anyone.*
> —*The Collapse of Evolution* by Scott M. Huse

The eye is the most complicated nanotechnological optical device in the known universe. Our eyes have 137 million light-receptive pixels in their retinas. The cone receptors in our eyes have chemicals sensitive to different wavelengths of light that our brain represents to us as colors. Even color is a God-given representation to us in our brains. The only scientific differences in light are the measure of its wavelength. The chemicals in the cones stimulate an electrochemical response that is transmitted over the optic nerve to our brains. This information is transmitted at least thirty times per second. In the brain, the information is reconstructed into a three-dimensional hologram of our surroundings replete with depth, color, brightness, and texture.   See *www.learnthebible.org*

Sometimes during the course of our time together, I will try to write with facts and build a case, so to speak. . . . Sometimes our visit will be more conversational. The main point again leads us to consider—power—and will. God has given us his creation to interface with. Everything that our five senses come in contact with, and some that we will never come in contact with. It is totally awesome and needs to be that way. We humans *seem to need* constant reminders of how awesome creation truly is. It is beyond our full powers of discovery and understanding, and yet God desires us to enjoy a lifetime of search and discovery. By so doing we may conclude that He is truly awesome. The revelation that he is awesome in power and yet personal is foundational in our relationship with Him.

God called the universe into being out of His own free will and by His absolute power, creating everything out of nothing. Let's look at a few of the scriptures that point us to that conclusion.

> a. *By the Word of the Lord were the heavens made . . .*
> *For He spoke and it came to be. . . . Psalm. 33:6,9*

 b. *But God made the earth by his power,*
  he founded the world by his wisdom,
  he stretched out the heavens by his understanding. Jeremiah.
  10:12

 c. *Through him all things were made; without him nothing*
  was made that has been made. John 1:3

 d. *For by him all things were created: things in heaven and*
  on earth, visible and invisible, whether thrones or powers
  or rulers or authorities: all things were created by him and
  for him. He is before all things, and in him all things hold
  together. Col 1:16,17

 e. *For by faith we understand that the universe was formed*
  *at God's **command**, so that what is seen was not made*
  out of visible. Hebrews 11:3 (my emphasis)

 f. *You are worthy our Lord and God, to receive glory and*
  honor and power, for you created all things, and by your
  ***will** they were created and have their being. Revelation*
  4:11 (my emphasis)

The Hebrew word to create *(bara)* is always used of God, never of man; it is the power to speak into existence that which had no prior existence.

1. To make *(asah)*, the ability to organize already existing matter into more complex systems—is used for both God and man. See Gen, 2:3

2. To form *(yatsar)*, the ability to form already existing matter into more structured objects—is also used in relation to both God and man.

There is no basis for saying that *bara* only means an instantaneous, out-of-nothing, supernatural creative action but that *asah* only means a slow, natural or God-guided process of making things out of existing material. In the creation account both words are used in reference to the *ex nihilo* creation event, and both are used in reference to things God made from previously existing material. The context of Genesis and the whole Bible seem overwhelmingly in favor of interpreting both *bara* and *asah* in Genesis 1 as virtually instantaneous acts.

I think "God spoke . . . let there be . . ." *and there was,* pretty much means **boom!** The thought I want to leave you with is that we somehow ought to lift up our minds to consider the awesome power of our Lord. Awesome even if some things were not made **in a New York minute**! Imagine if any one of us was able to speak, and by the power of his or her will, the miracle of a child came into being? Would we then taunt them? "Sure, but it took you long enough. I mean *nine months!*" While obviously, I like to picture my God making things happen in an instant, it is His sheer **will and power** that made them manifest. I admit I don't have near enough faith to think he started the slimy idea some billions of years ago. . . . But that is not the larger impression I want to make.

What do you think? Has anything caused you to ponder something you may not have considered before? Is there anything that particularly "grinds your gears" that you want to write down to ask me about or look up on your own? Please write it here in this space. Okay?

I want you to take with this chapter the theme of **power, will, and consequences!**

In each chapter, near or at the end, I want to leave room for something very important. Please. This is not a long book. Enjoy the journey. I know you could read it quickly, but I think we would all grow and benefit from some time for reflection and reaction.

Time well spent:

What did you think of that simplistic Garden of Eden picture a few pages ago?

If there was such a place, what was it like?

What systems of dating are used today? Are they reliable or infallible?

Do you agree that everybody has a worldview?

Please explain.

What scripture verse from this chapter stuck with you most?

The Roman Coliseum, originally known as the *Flavian Amphitheatre*, is an elliptical amphitheatre in the center of Rome, Italy that is the largest stadium built by the mighty Roman Empire. The Coliseum is considered one of the greatest works of Roman architecture ever built. Originally capable of seating 50,000 spectators, it was once used for gladiatorial combat.

The construction of the Colosseum began under the rule of Roman Emperor Vespasian around 72 A.D. and was completed by his son, Titus, in the 80s A.D. It was built at the site of Nero's lake below his extensive palace, the Domus Aurea, which had been built covering the slope of the Palatine after the great fire of Rome in 64 A.D. Dio Cassius said that 10,000 wild animals were killed in the one hundred days of celebration which inaugurated the amphitheatre opening. The arena floor was covered with sand, presumably to soak the blood and make it easier to clean away.

The Colosseum hosted large-scale spectacular games that included fights between animals, the killing of prisoners by animals and other executions, naval battles (via flooding the arena and bringing in ships) up until 81 A.D., and combats between gladiators *(munera)*. The *munera* were always given by private individuals rather than the state. It has been estimated that several hundreds of thousands died in the Colosseum games. See *www.biblestudy.org*

Please read the above description again.

What would you feel if your favorite sports team proposed to build a stadium like that these days?

Do you think we could pull it off?

What kind of human will lead the way in building such an amazing complex?

Do you think that WILL understood it would be used for torture and persecution?

Chapter 2

Of Sheets and Stadiums:
the gift of free will

*I*f you have an important message to communicate, how is it best to get it across? Some write it on banners trailing behind planes that fly up and down the beach trying to sell seafood or skydiving. Some may plaster the sides of our roadways or buildings with billboards that block out the view.

Do you know what I don't recall seeing as much as I used to? Sheets. That's right, sheets. Remember when you might go to or watch a football game and there would be, (often more than one) sheets with words painted on them hanging over the railing. I don't recall seeing my favorite one in quite some time: John 3:16. Have you ever wondered about why somebody would choose that particular verse? What is it about that verse that might make it a very good choice for that short window of opportunity to communicate their very important message?

That demonstration has a message about free will and communication on several different levels. Some people are offended by it. More than just being part and parcel of the right to freedom of speech, it can seem to some as a violation of space. Personal space—mental space. Just one word and a few simple numbers can mean so much! Seems much less intrusive than the guy who almost poked my eye out with the section of picket fence he made out of cardboard! If you're not a football fan you won't get that one.

So, here we are. We have a worldview we want to share. We are going to a game where the likelihood is that a large number of people might be influenced by this message we feel needs to be heard. But, why that one particular scripture? Why not another classic favorite? Leviticus 21:19 . . . You know . . . "festering or running sores. . . ." Kidding! You know you want to look it up. Anyway, back to our sheet. A scripture! At a ball game! From the BIBLE! You mean some people take that old book so seriously that they mess up a sheet just to write that on it, then lug it through security and hang it on the fence? Wow! Fan—atics!

My wife is a teacher and a very good one at that. When she wants to get a point across to make it easier to comprehend or retain, she sometimes goes into "rap-mode." Oh yeah . . . She stands before her children and gets all funky and starts sayin', "brreak it down—oooh—ahh . . . brreak it down—oooh—ahh." Then she starts dissecting the sentence or grammar or equation. It works well and, besides, she looks even cuter than normal. Given that technique I learned, permit me to take that scripture . . . no (knucklehead), not Leviticus, but John 3:16 . . .without the rap!

I think there are many things that can be drawn out of this one passage.

For God so loved the world that he gave his one and only Son, that whoever believes in him will not perish but have eternal life.

—John 3:16

a. For GOD:

This identifies the Who—the power, the initiator of what follows. This is the God I was telling you about in the first chapter. The one who is more powerful, more majestic, more awesome than anything your mortal brain can wrap itself around. He is the God of all creation, of all government, of all time, space, and matter.

*** TIME OUT *** Hey, I said we were at a game! This is a good time for a time out. AKA . . . important announcement.

In 2004 George Bush, the then president of the United States, made a statement that struck me as odd. I must also warn you that going down this particular bunny trail has caused a few people to lose their heads—*literally!*

In an exclusive interview with ABC News' Charles Gibson, Bush said he believes both Christians and Muslims worship the same God. He stated "We have different routes of getting to the Almighty . . . I want you to understand, I want your listeners to understand, I don't get to decide who goes to heaven." Do Christians and Muslims worship the same God? I will say no more regarding President Bush, and I give him credit for reverence . . . saying the Almighty is better than *the Man Upstairs* . . . but the fact is, he and millions are wrong.

Here are just a few things that can easily be gleaned when doing a study on World Religions. Suppose that the following summary is accurate:

- Mohammed is the founder of the religion of Islam. Islam means *surrender or submission* It is more about surrender to the will of Allah than it is about believing.
- The Arabian people were polytheistic and had a pantheon of deities (including Allah—also thought to be the Moon God).
- Mohammed was disturbed by the idolatrous practices of his countrymen and came to the conclusion that Allah was the one true God. He became intensely monotheistic. Since Allah is the one true God, the Christian doctrine of the Trinity is then polytheistic. God had or has no sons. This makes it more than a little difficult to accept the doctrine of the Trinity which is essential to sound Christian doctrine. It also makes things a bit dicey when trying to decide then what to do with Jesus' claim to be God and that **no man can come to God except through Him!**
- Allah has sent many prophets (some place the number at over 100,000) to guide men. The Koran mentions twenty-eight of these, most of whom are found in the Old and New Testaments. Jesus is said to be a sinless prophet, but Mohammed is the last and greatest of the prophets.
- Of the four inspired books, the Koran is the most important. The other three are the Tauret (that's the Pentateuch—the first five books of the Bible), the Zabur (the Psalms of David), and The Injil (Four

Gospels of Jesus). So—if Muslims recognize these books of the Christian Bible and even at one time called Christians and Jews "people of the book," why is it that some can dismiss these same people as infidels, and wish them a pleasant explosion? It is because they simply believe that the early revelations are in corrupted form and the Koran supersedes them. The Koran is held to be as eternal as Allah. It was simply dictated to Mohammed by Gabriel over a period of years.

Again, I do not mean to pick on President Bush nor do I wish to pick a fight with Islam. I only ask the reader to consider what would happen in the Arab world if one of their leaders stood up and said Allah is the same God as the Jewish or Christian God. Gives new meaning to "heads will roll." "Just sayin." ☺ *** TIME IN ***

b. So Loved:
This identifies God's basic characteristic. This awesome, unmatched, creator of the universe uses this active verb right off the bat. And when you study the word used to describe God's love used throughout the New Testament it is called "*Agape.*" This is the deepest and purest form of love possible. The kind of love that is selfless, giving, and which gives freely of itself with no thought of getting anything in return. The kind of love that would make someone lay down their life for another. *** TIME OUT ***

Did you know that there are several kinds of love? Here at the stadium during today's game, I'm quite

sure you overheard examples of some of them. Yep. . . .
When number eighty-five came running on the field
and took off his helmet I heard somebody say that he
is the older brother of number thirty-two. You can see
they resemble each other and it is obvious that they
love (Greek word *Phileo*) each other. Another person
said that the fact is, that most everybody in the crowd
has come to these games for years whether they win
or lose. They love (Greek word *Storge*) their fellow
fans as much as they do "Da Bears." And you! . . .
When the cheerleaders passed by I saw you look them
over, and when you saw that blonde, you even said,
"I think I'm in love." (Greek word *Eros*). By the way,
the English translation is "you can buy me a hot dog
'cause I know you are married and I know where you
live." ☺ *** TIME IN ***

Sometime go to your Bible and read 1 Corinthians 13.
That is often called the "love chapter." Every time the
word love is used it is the *agape* kind of love. A good word
picture for the way God loves us would be to substitute
the word God in the verse in place of each instance love
is used. God is patient, God is kind, and so on.

c. The World:
This identifies the recipient of this pure, everlasting
love. We know that this word comes from the Greek
word *Kosmos*. We also know for sure that the Bible is
not talking primarily about things created or things
that can be accumulated. Nor is it talking about the
world system, "the Matrix", if you will. The world that

God loves is the world of humankind, the apple of his eye. This is the object clearly identified in John 3:16. We humans, on the other hand, can and do love all manner of things, objects, idols; real or imagined. We slave our lives away, often hoarding things that have no eternal life or lasting value. And we—we who go under the banner of Christian—are told to seek out, and lavishly love, this same world. But it's a world that is in darkness and desperately needs to walk in the true and liberating light.

d. That He Gave:

This awesome God gives us another verb to show us more about his character. "Are you kidding? He still has not asked one thing from us!" Correct. If we consider and somehow grasp a little of how infinite God is and we couple that with some appreciation for the depth and power of his love, is it any wonder that we don't have much we can give him? I am not saying that what he desires from us and what we truly can give is insignificant! Remember trying to buy something for your dad for Christmas when you were little? What do you get for the man who has everything, for the guy who has shirts older than you? In fact, that is a good picture of us and our Heavenly Father. We might go buy Dad a card or a wrench with money he gave us for allowance. Maybe we weren't able to do that. Maybe Mommy took us to the store and the only thing we could do is *choose* the gift. Maybe one of the biggest gifts we can give our Heavenly Father is to choose to love him and honor him!

e. His One and Only Son:

The One perfect in power and perfect in love could give nothing less than the perfect Gift to his creation. Because he loves us, he knows us intimately, he knows what we need most. We are a broken and lost people. We are most in need of a redeemer. We need that more than we need all the things we chase after. We even need that more than we need the things that our hearts are hurting for. If indeed John 3:16 is a foundational passage in God's love letter to us, if indeed it is one of the most important scriptures we could use on our sheet, so to speak,—then this Gift that this whole scripture has pointed us to has to be HUGE.

There is one way that can help us identify if another religion or belief system is cultish, or false, or divisive. That is simply . . . what does it do with this Gift spoken of in scripture? What do they do with Jesus?

Do they:

- Ignore the Gift? Say that he was never born or lived on this earth?
- Do they say he was just a prophet, one of many come and gone?
- Do they say he was a god, and we too can become gods?
- Do they diminish or deny what he clearly said about himself?

I certainly did not talk about our Muslim friends earlier to single them out and make it appear they are exclusive in some of their doctrine that would identify them as not being a Christian sect or faith system. God's word is the article that has drawn the line in the sand. His word states that the Son that he gave is equal to God . . . His word tells us that Jesus is the one who said that no one can come to the Father unless they come through him (Jesus). While God's word and desire is totally inclusive of all mankind, it is exclusive and jealous about how that result can happen. Never lose sight of the fact that we are not to compromise the message of this Gift. We are to present this gift to all mankind using love, the testimony of our lives, and sound doctrine as our method and tools. It has brought hatred, resentment, and corruption when it has been presented or brought using other methods such as the Crusades or 'Manifest Destiny' for example.

f. That Whoever Believes in **Him:**
Just as there is only one great Gift, there is only one way to receive it. It is to BELIEVE. We will develop this more later as it is critical to our theme of power and will in this book. God essentially tells us in this scripture what he wants back. We are his children. We are his creation. He doesn't need another tie or wrench. We are too small to help him pay the taxes or the mortgage on the house. These are symbolic of our relationship to our Father, but even they fall short in that, God never has lack, he is never in need or want. Our axiom of two sure things in life—death and taxes—doesn't phase him a bit! In short, to receive the Gift—believe the Gift.

g. Will Not Perish but Have Eternal Life:
This is the culmination of the whole passage. I do not
want to get caught up in arguments about heaven or
hell.—Does it exist or not?
Are there literal flames and a lake of fire? Nor do I want
to speculate about heaven. Are there really gates of pearl,
streets of gold, and a mansion with an attached garage,
four-wheeler, or fifty virgins? Sorry for the sarcasm—kind
of! I want us just to revel in this promise of eternal life.
If I have believed John 3:16 up to this point, this awesome, creative, loving God and I will have eternal life!
You know what? That makes me feel like he wants a
relationship with me! I get it! I think he really does
love me and wants a relationship with me. I think if
that is really the case, I am going to get started with it
now—while I'm down here.
Badda Bing—Badda BOOM!!

*** TIME OUT *** The chapter is almost over and we have
one to use up! Our boys are finally down in the red zone!

Maybe one way we can look at the significance of John 3:16
would be to write it another way. The following way is an example
of how it has been written all through human history when man
has been in charge and had his or her way. Please bear with the
use of the smiley faces. I know they will one day date this writing,
but sometimes when one steps on toes they can be helpful. I really
hope you read through this paragraph example more than once.
Feel free to insert your own descriptive words as they come to mind.
If you are a student of world history, or even a follower of current
events, you may agree with the assertions I am trying to make.

Hitler . . . (you can insert here any name you like—despot, president, evil henchman ☺) . . . so ruled . . . (you might say governed, lorded over, dominated) . . . the world . . . (insert here—empire, corporation, sometimes wife and kids ☺) . . . that he . . . (demanded, required, taxed, coerced, raped and plundered) . . . his only . . . (ambassador, pawn, expendable representative) . . . that whoever . . . (serves, measures up, gives up, or sucks up ☺) . . . will have . . . (however long it takes to bleed out, or perpetuate his agenda).

Does that sound cynical? I suppose so. I believe mankind is the apple of God's eye, his prized creation and masterpiece. But I guess I don't believe in the inherent basic goodness of man or his "god-self" buried within. I know he cannot love with *agape* love unless the Spirit of God lives within him and history seems to bear this out. Just sayin'. ☺ *** TIME IN ***

The theme again of this book is about **power** and **will** and consequence. In this case the God of infinite **power** exercised his **will** which was to love us and have a relationship with us. It resulted in the consequence of our being able to have eternal life and an eternal home!

There is power in will . . . it does have consequences . . . and if it was given or built within us ANY way other than as FREE WILL, I hate to say, we would have to insert the Lord's name in place of Hitler in the above example. And don't think for a minute that because God knows and controls everything in the course of human affairs, that we must be predestined to either accept or reject him, thus having no free will! That is for another break in the action and we are flat out of time outs. ☺

Time well spent:

Do you think we all kind of have the same God?

Is the Bible too exclusive? Should it be?

Who do you 'agape?' Why?

When was the last time you saw a sign or sheet with John 3:16 displayed?

Would you be embarrassed if I brought a sheet to the game with you and me?

Do you think there were any messages posted at the Roman stadium I showed you earlier?

Chapter 3

A Flash and a Fall:
I will be God

We have spent quite a great deal of time making a case for the magnitude of God, his creation, and his freely given Gift. I wonder if we might just switch gears for a few minutes and take a quick pop survey. I called it a survey because it is not a quiz in the sense that you will be graded, or that there are exact answers for each question. An antonym is a word that is used as the opposite in meaning as it relates to another. Suppose a game show used this format? You must match each word with a word that you feel is the opposite. Each answer is worth one thousand dollars.

Here we go.

1. Hot: _____

2. Fast: _____

3. Up: _____

4. Long: _____

5. War: _____

6. Love: _____

7. God: _____

Did you answer all seven? You understand that you have the possibility of earning $7,000? Before we answer these I just want to ask you if you would risk a bonus round? The bonus round is for an undisclosed reward if you decide that any one of these words does not have an opposite. Did your answers look similar to the following? 1. cold. 2. slow. 3. down. 4. short 5. peace 6. hate 7. Satan.

I suppose most people would have similar answers for the above questions. If you are a Christian I do not want to offend you, but I surely hope you weren't tricked into answering number seven with the answer Satan? Let me explain. If I were to give you a question above that asked you to give an answer opposite to the word universe, what would you have said? We get the idea right off that the universe is humongous. What could we have groped for as an answer? Maybe sand? Maybe dust? Maybe electron? What is our concept of God? I doubt that if we were to give a similar quiz to our Muslim friend—asking "What is the opposite of Allah?"—that he would have even considered Satan. Why is our concept of our God Jehovah sometimes so small? God has no opposite. There is nothing and no-one he can be compared to! By the way—the "bonus round" was a hypothetical test of character. If we had the idea that Satan was not the opposite of God, but answered that just because we felt the majority would had done so . . . or worse yet to collect

$7000, then we might deserve that "undisclosed reward"—(and it probably is not a pleasant one!)

Well then, who is this person or entity of fame and history. Satan was a created being. We spoke earlier that in Colossians we are told that God created all powers, thrones, rulers, principalities, and authorities. All were made by Him and for Him. Satan was no exception. It is true that Satan once had great power before the throne of God. He was not the opposite of good. He was not the "dark side of the Force," for that too could cause one to think of Jehovah as the Good side—equal—but good. Nor was he one half of the Yin and the Yang.

The Bible tells us much about Lucifer, which is Latin for "light bearer." We find accounts in Isaiah as well as in the book of Ezekiel of this created being. Lucifer was the anointed cherub. Anointed means to be set apart for God's divine purpose. God had given Lucifer a certain amount of power and authority. Lucifer wanted to exalt himself above God, rather than "just" being the favored angel of God.

Lucifer was created perfect in all his ways, but iniquity was found in him. Like man, angels were created perfect, and with a free will. Be careful not to think that perfect means equal to God. It means complete. He must have been beautiful, and majestic, enjoying constant access to the throne of God.

> *"You were the model of perfection, full of wisdom and perfect in beauty. You were in Eden, the garden of God; every precious stone adorned you: ruby, topaz and emerald, chrysolite, onyx and jasper, sapphire, turquoise and*

*beryl. Your settings and mountings were made of gold; on the day **you were created** they were prepared. You were the anointed as a guardian cherub, for I ordained you. You were on the holy mount of God; you walked among the fiery stones. You were blameless from the day **you were created** till wickedness was found in you.*
—Ezekiel 28:12-15 (my emphasis)

God created a beautiful being, an archangel who gathered up praise and worship before the throne of God. Music was formed in and through him. Lucifer knew all there was to know about worship. That is why he is effective many times in getting people away from worshiping God in spirit and truth. His rebellious spirit infects Christians. That spirit sometimes causes movements and churches to split because of disagreements over the emphasis in the form of worship.

We know from scripture that Lucifer did not continue on in the presence or favor of God. What kind of authority did he once possess that he actually thought he could somehow take it as his own to become equal to God? And what position did he enjoy in heaven that would allow him so much power and influence that he would take a third of all the angels into rebellion with him? Lastly—and what follows our looking into power, will and consequence—what could have happened that forever determined his future?

I suppose now is as good a time as any to ask you to consider along with me something that rises out of the theme and discussion of this book. Looking at your life as a whole, can you think of an event or a determination you made that forever changed the course or future of your life? I know that if I were to be totally candid with you, I could tell you for certain of instances that I chose to follow a course or do something and nothing remained quite the same thereafter.

As I mentioned earlier I believe that some events happen rather suddenly. I also have tried to build a case for the greatness of God. Going back to the time of creation, in my imagination, I have a hard time believing that around the "drawing board" of God there lay a bunch of crumpled up plans and designs. Although many things seem bizarre to me and some totally unnecessary (i.e. the mosquito), they are fascinating and complex. Each one somehow serves a purpose in the grand scheme of things. Some resemble other forms of creations, and yet are distinct and marvelous. I believe that about as suddenly as these facets of creation entered the mind and wisdom of God—he spoke them into existence.

Now then—what do we do about this "pesky" archangel? The Bible tells us he was in rebellion. We know that he did something to cause disruption in both heaven and earth. Let's look at what the prophet Isaiah tells us.

> You said in your heart,
>   "I will ascend to heaven;
>   I will raise my throne above the stars of God;
>   I will sit enthroned on the mount of assembly,
>   on the utmost
>   heights of the sacred mountain.
>   I will ascend above the tops of the clouds;
>   I will make myself like the Most High.
>   —Isaiah 14:13,14 (my emphasis)

So what was God's response? Did he call a meeting? Maybe thought about sending Lucifer to "time out" until he cooled off, or until God could figure out how to salvage this threat to his classroom control. Might it be a good idea at this time to threaten this angel with probation? Or, maybe it would be wise to partner and join forces. . . . I mean . . . some people and religions like to think we can be equal? . . . (Kidding here, of course) This is a classic demonstration of the POWER of "I WILL" . . . and the consequences. Five times Satan put his fist in God's face declaring "I will." Ready? Ready? Hold on . . . wait for it. BOOM! **In a New York minute!** "You're outta here, bub." Or in this case Beelzebub. I mean . . . how do you get kicked out of heaven slowly . . . is there such a thing as a slow flash?

> *How you have fallen from heaven, O morning star, son of the dawn! You have been cast down to the earth.*
> —Isaiah 14:12

> *So I drove you in disgrace from the mount of God, and I expelled you, O guardian cherub, from the fiery stones. So I threw you to the earth.*
> —Ezekiel 28:16,17

> *I saw Satan fall like lightning from heaven.*
> —Luke 10:18

I especially like the last scripture reference. Jesus talks in the first person there in Luke. He was there at the time of the fall. Jesus is not some created being. He is not a prophet. He is Son of the Most High, equal partner in the Trinity of the Father, Son, and Holy Spirit. He never claimed, like Satan, that he would be like God, nor did he claim that he was or would become, as is the case in many religions, a god. He tells all mankind that he is

God, that he and the Father are one. He was not cast down and out . . . but rules and reigns!

Time well spent:

Do you think many people believe there is an entity called Satan?

How much influence does he have in your life?

He is called the god of this world. What does he really affect or control?

What do you think?

How big was the company of angels that fell with Satan?

Where were they, or are they now?

What do they do?

Chapter 4

The Apple Doesn't Fall Far From the Tree:
I will be like God

*R*ecipe for confusion: Take a universe that is mind boggling in its creative diversity, complexity and function. Add the fact that God states that his whole nature is love and that creation was made for his pleasure. Then honestly look at the situation mankind is in locally and globally! (You can even take into account the way you look and feel first thing in the morning!) The end result of this recipe might be a heaping dish of "Whatzupwiththat?"

Earlier I explained that Satan was a created being, with a free will—and with power. Man too is a created being, with free will—and power. But he was created in the image of God. Genesis tells us that God said: (that is the Father, the Son, and the Holy Spirit) "Let **us** make man in our image." The Hebrew word used for God in Genesis 1:26 is *Elohiym*. It is a plural noun and it is used three times with the singular verb *bara* that I spoke about earlier.

God created man perfect. He was not in any way equal to God, but was complete and lacking nothing. God is spirit (John 4:24). Man resembles God in many aspects. Man is a tripartite being. He is made up of soul, body, and spirit. He possesses an immortal spirit. He has a soul, out of which comes his ability the think, feel, decide, and make choices. He is creative, was made for work, purpose, and destiny.

I would never try to tell you that Satan is not powerful. He is, after all, referred to as the *god of this world*. He has the ability to exert much of his twisted and limited authority over the affairs of man for the time being. His power is finite though. He used his free will to essentially earn the consequences of his rebellion. This is a tangent, but have you ever heard anyone ask, "If God is love, how could he send Satan to a place of separation and damnation?" Of course not! We have heard it said often enough about a departed person, but never where the devil is concerned. How could he send anyone to Hell? He freely chose separation. Free will has consequences as we shall continue to see.

Have you ever thought of man, for instance Adam, as a powerful being? Let's consider Adam at the time of his creation. He was created perfect. He was created to live forever in **fellowship** with God. (As it was—the Bible records him as living 930 years.) Adam was the beloved steward of God's creation. We can also see a little of the humility of God in Genesis. After he made man in his image, he stated that man's purpose was to **rule over** the fish of the sea and the birds of the air, over all livestock, and over all the earth! God made it, which was no small feat!—and then backed up to give authority to rule it to this unproven "man-unit." Furthermore we see evidence of the great fellowship God had with Adam in the following passage:

Now the Lord God had formed out of the ground all the beasts of the field and all the birds of the air. **He brought them to the man to see what** <u>he would</u> **name them;** *and whatever the man called each living creature, that was its name. So the man gave names to all the livestock, the birds of the air, and the beasts of the field.*

—Gen 2:19,20 *(my emphasis)*

We must not look at Adam out of our glasses of human experience. We subliminally think of him (at least we do if we're men) as being of average height and weight . . . able to bench your own weight, maybe do a couple of chin-ups, always remembers when to rotate the tires!—Or (if we're a woman), we'd be a multi-tasking ball of screamin' beauty, strength, and stamina. ☺ just sayin'. . . . Imagine this Adam the next time you try to remember back to high school biology. Now was it phylum, or species, or genotype? Adam named them all, and my guess is (after she was created), Eve not only knew them, but had nicknames for each. So great was the mental prowess of man. Everything at that time was unpolluted, uncompromised, unbroken! Don't think of soul-power as only mind or memory. I think Adam's power of influence as well as perception and cognition were far greater than our present ability. If you find this at all interesting, you might also enjoy studying about the latent power of the soul by people such as Watchman Nee.

In an earlier scene we were in a stadium and from time to time took a brief time out. This time we are in a Garden and I ask your permission to go down a short "bunny trail." PS, The name "bunny" was Eve's idea!

On occasion, after I have made a friendly connection with some teens or young people, I ask them if they know what "STDs" are. Of course, they have learned all about STDs from, high school health class or maybe even an adult family member or mentor. Consequently they roll their eyes as if to say, "Like Duh!" or "do we have to go there?" I usually get their attention and thoughtfulness when I tell them I am talking about a whole different kind of S T D. I call it "Soul Tie Disease." You see I think our souls, though diminished in their capacity a great deal since Adam's day, are still very powerful. I also believe the Bible when it tells us that when two people become one, most commonly through sexual relations, that they become one flesh. Something profound, real, and somewhat mystical happens. Something of their very essence—their soul—their very being, becomes one with that other person. In God's plan it is not uncommon to see married couples that become extraordinarily connected and even somewhat similar over time, and this is according to God's design and plan. They often finish each others thoughts or sentences; they may know the other's unspoken request or desire before it is expressed; and sad to say, sometimes they know innately or intuitively when the other one has not been faithful to them. In my counseling experience, I have seen the soul tie disease break up families and relationships, sometimes when years or even decades have passed; when after two people have been married, the "scent" or soul tie of another, earlier affair is so powerful that they abandon conscience and commitment. Usually the consequences of that freely-willed choice are tragic for everyone involved.

Back to the Garden.

Now we have perfect Adam and his perfect mate in the Garden of Eden. And let's quickly look at the following if you are inclined to think that Adam and Eve were only creatures of myth. The first genealogy in Chronicles—indisputably an historical book—begins with Adam in a historical sense. Likewise Adam is mentioned in Christ's genealogy in Luke 3:38, and by Jude in relation to a historical Enoch. Jesus talks about how God made Adam and Eve, making them male and female, and said that "for this cause a man shall leave his father and mother and become one flesh." Here in Matthew 19:4-5 he ties Genesis 1 and Genesis 2 together, quoting them as history.

Something is not free unless there is a test, or some means to compare it against. This couple had a free, unhindered relationship to God. But, as we have stated, they were created with free will. The test was so easy. Man was told he could eat of EVERY fruit of the Garden, except one. God could have been stingy and really tested their limits by saying, "you can eat of only one tree and you better stay away from all the rest."

The test hinged on one thing only. The choice would determine whether man would submit to God. Would he be content to be stay perfect (complete and lacking nothing), or would he try to exalt his will above God's? In the story of the Fall of mankind I am reminded of Psalm 1:

> *Blessed is the man who does not walk in the counsel of the wicked, or stand in the way of sinners, or sit in the seat of mockers.*

The path of sin is often a progressive one. First we listen (counsel) to what we should not. Before long we find ourselves slowed down and stopping forward progress (standing) in our walk with the Lord. Then we actually abide (sit) down in the midst of our sin and folly.

The serpent (Satan) was crafty and deceitful and said to the woman:

> *Did God really say 'You must not eat from the tree of the garden?' The woman said to the serpent, 'We may eat of the trees in the garden, but God said, 'You must not eat fruit from the tree that is in the middle of the garden, and you must not touch it, or you will die.'*

> *'You will not surely die,' the serpent said to the woman, 'For God knows that when you eat of it your eyes will be opened, and you will be like God, knowing good and evil.'*

> *When the woman saw that the fruit of the tree was **good for food** and **pleasing to the eye,** and **desirable for gaining wisdom,** she took some and ate it. She also gave some to her husband <u>who was with her</u>, and he ate it. The eyes of both of them were opened, and they realized they were naked.*
>
> —Genesis 3:1-7 *(my emphasis)*

There is truly so much we can draw from these scriptures that applies to our faith. Notice even how the areas of appeal coincide with those described in 1 John 2:16. Eve saw that the tree was:

Good for food . . . . the lust of the flesh
Pleasing to the eyes . . . . the lust of the eyes
Desirable for gaining wisdom . . . . the pride of life

Scripture tells us that Eve was deceived, but lays the blame on Adam and charges the consequences to him. Because of the sin of ONE MAN! Well, what happened? God must have been grieved. He had gone to all this trouble to create a being that would be the pinnacle of his creative genius; a creation that he could have constant fellowship with; a being that he could pour out his essence upon—love completely and eternally.

God did not fall to pieces, but He also didn't ignore the consequences, restructure the parameters or change the rules. Adam, and Eve, were creatures of power . . . who had a free will. The power of "I will" had consequences. I believe it was at that moment when they both knew what they were doing and followed through with it, that both their and our history was changed. In a "New York minute" sin and death entered the human race. It may have not been a "**boom**" flash, like when Satan was cast out of heaven. The word picture I might liken it to is "**boom**" and the plug is pulled in the bathtub drain. Immediately the effects of the act were started in place. Just as it may take quite some time for the water to drain from the tub, it will drain. The water will be gone . . . dissipate. The glory that once was man, the strength and perfection, would wane and is still waning to this day. What was immediate though has even more eternal ramifications and sadness. The spirit of man was IMMEDIATELY broken from God. This was not different from the immediate separation and forever broken fellowship God had with Satan. . . . Except, PRAISE GOD; he had a way of redemption already laid. Because his character is LOVE, he would not allow us to **remain** separated from him unless it is OUR CHOICE!

"Adam and Eve Driven Out of Eden" *by Gustave Doré*

So he drove out the man; and he placed at the east of the garden of Eden
Cherubim, and a flaming sword which turned every way, to keep the way of
the tree of life. —Gen 3:24

WHAT IS SIN?

Sin entered the world through the fall of Satan. And now sin
had entered into mankind through the test, failure, and fall of

Adam. Technically the word sin means "missing the mark." That doesn't sound good, but it sounds textbook-like, not something real or tangible. I believe it is as real as DNA or things we deal with that our senses can perceive. But I also believe that belief is real, that it has force and effect. I cannot explain either and can only propose this to you for consideration. The sociologist might call sin "cultural lag." The psychiatrist terms it "self-destructive behavior." The philosopher names it 'irrational thinking." The humanist excuses it as "human weakness." The Marxist defines it as "class struggle."

> *Therefore, just as sin entered the world through one man, and death through sin; and in this way death came to all men because all sinned.*
>
> —Romans 5:12

Sin entered the human race as certainly as a cancer cell spreads throughout the whole body. Adam and Eve were cast out of the Garden. Fellowship was broken. There was hostility (enmity) between Adam and his beloved Eve. There was fear and trembling, mistrust between them and God. The ground they worked was now cursed. The dominion over animal life was made more difficult. Since I cannot prove what sin is and it is so very hard to wrap our finite (five senses) mind around such a concept, may I just "wax an elephant" about the topic and leave the judgment to the reader to accept, reject as absurdity, or research on their own about the matter?

I understand and accept to be true some of the following:

1. Adam and Eve had intimate fellowship with God.
2. They lived in a paradise environment.
3. He named and knew all plants and animals.

4. There was no sickness or disease.
5. Adam lived to be over 900 years old.
6. If sin had not entered the human condition he would have lived forever.

Now I would like to put in a paragraph what I see the condition of the world to be in our life and time. Most people have no, let alone an intimate, fellowship with God. Many people live in apathy, rebellion, fear of God, with many mad at God. We live in a world of violence, weather extremes and tragedy. There are many parts of it that are poisonous to us in their form or nature; some are toxic to us because of our carelessness, i.e., pollution. Many types of plants and animals have become extinct, and many of the animals we interact with can be hostile or threatening. We spend billions fighting devastating plagues and disease. We know all so well what sickness has done to our own bodies and grieve over what it has done to our loved ones. The life expectancy is nowhere near what it was for Adam, Eve and many figures in genealogy. The gene pool has been weakened, diluted, and mutated from its original purity. We face a certain death, and run like madmen hiding from its reality.

May I ask anyone to explain something to me? How could something so innocent and benign, as we usually think of sin to be, produce even a few of the above very tangible results? I don't understand it myself, and if I did, I would probably be more apt to ask, "Why is it that I don't more readily embrace the cure that is also there in scripture?" While I don't necessarily believe that specific sin patterns or sinful traits are passed down to each subsequent generation in families, I do believe that the sin nature is passed down, that sin is real and that if you or I were the original people in the Garden and were told to "stay away from that one tree" . . .

I probably would have been climbing in it just to get to a certain especially ripe one—or shaking the branches to knock some down for you! That is one reason I used the "apple doesn't fall very far from the tree" in the title of the chapter. We are so much like our forefathers. The stage props vary with different eras, cultures and races, but the basic human condition remains the same.

There is one more thing I would like to bring out from this short study in Genesis that is relevant. I would like you to consider that just as Adam and Eve were the progenitors of sinful mankind, they were also the founding fathers of religion!

Remember, Adam and Eve walked perfectly (complete) in unbroken fellowship and **innocent relationship** with God. That is what God wants so dearly for us now and has made a way for through Christ Jesus. There was no strain in the relationship. God showed his trust and friendship with man by letting him name and rule over all creation. Soon after the fall and sin had entered into the heart of man, religion soon followed. Religion is man's way of reaching God, appeasing him, placating him, covering up, and governing ourselves. We are told in scripture that God made garments "of flesh" (Genesis 3:21) to cover man's nakedness. Even in this we see God's love. He made the garments. Something had to die because of *their* sin, not because of God's requirements, and blood had to be shed. We still today see religions of all kind with elaborate robes and attire. God never required this at first when it was about relationship! Next we see in Genesis 4 that sacrifices started to be practiced.

"In the course of time Cain brought some of the fruits of the soil as an offering to the Lord. But Abel brought fat portions from some of the firstborn of his flock."

—Genesis 4:3, 4

I do not want us to get caught up in how the offerings were received by the Lord. I also can hear some people saying, "But what about the Levitical law? What about all that religion that God himself laid out for Moses?" That is not the point here, and if we know our scripture, we know that it was not the blood of goats and bulls the Lord wanted, nor was it strict obedience to the rules and regulations set forth. The point of the Law was to show man it is IMPOSSIBLE to please the Lord or have intimate fellowship with him by human striving or human reasoning. Never forget that in the Old Testament the Lord clearly told man what was the most important thing that he asked of mankind, and just so we would not miss the point, Jesus repeated it in the New Testament. We are to love the Lord our God with all our heart . . . and then love our neighbor as ourself. That speaks clearly of relationship.

Remember what the devil told Eve? He reasoned with her and deceived her into believing that it was possible to become "like God." Remember that Satan wanted to become like God and take his place? Is it any wonder that he has tried to get mankind to follow in his own failed footsteps?

It might be a good opportunity for a break, so here comes another "bunny trail" while we finish up here in the Garden! Let's see if there are similarities in religions of the world that take us further from the true relationship God wanted, and still desires to have with us. Let's take just a short look at some of the many religions both East and West that collectively, have influenced multi-millions, if not billions of people.

Hinduism:
- Based upon ancient Upanishad tradition.
- Thousands upon thousands of gods and goddesses.

- Through numerous reincarnations one can become like God. One can break away from this wheel of *karma* when one realizes his soul *(Atman)* becomes identical with the universal soul *(Brahman)*
- There is no recognition of sin and moral guilt. Sin is an illusion. In his ultimate sense, man is God. He is therefore not separated from God by his sin.
- Hinduism is a works system. Forgiveness of sin does not fit into the picture of karma. There is a slow, evolving process of reaching "IT."

Buddhism:
- Founded upon the teachings of Siddhartha Gautama.
- Built upon the Four Noble Truths and the Eightfold Path.
- No sin—the Eightfold Path is more a system of "therapy" designed to develop habits which will release people from the restrictions caused by ignorance and cravings (desires).
- No form of Buddhism has a place for the biblical doctrines of God, man, sin, salvation, or resurrection. Most Buddhist sects are either polytheistic, pantheistic or even atheistic.
- When people are totally *Enlightened* they will finally attain *Nirvana* being freed from further rebirth and from the law of karma.

Taoism:
- Mystical Chinese religion founded by Lao-tsu.
- There is no personal Creator-God in any form of Taoism. Taoism is instead involved with nature, mysticism and impersonal principle.
- The issue of sin and morality is minimized in Taoism. Salvation is achieved by following the Tao (the Way).

- There are many gods, deities and evil spirits.

Mormonism:
- Founded around 1820 by Joseph Smith.
- Christ's deity is minimized by Mormons. Christ was a spirit child from one of the eternal spirit-gods. He is the spirit brother of Lucifer.
- Salvation is a progression toward becoming a god. When a man attains godhood, he is able to create and populate worlds of his own, so that the process can continue on forever.
- Elevates the writings of Joseph Smith above those of the Bible.
- Has changed its position a few times already (since polygamy bothers some people, and referring to African Americans as cursed, or mud people is not exactly politically correct lately!!!)

Jehovah's Witnesses:
- Founded in the late 1800s by Charles Taze Russell.
- Deny or distort almost every significant biblical truth, including the Trinity, the deity of Christ, the Virgin Birth, etc.
- Hold their *New World Translation* to be the only accurate rendition of scripture.
- Jesus is only "a god" and was once Michael the archangel and captain of Jehovah's hosts.

See Reflection Ministries Inc. Kenneth Boa

As we come back from this "bunny trail" I know you might be confused. After all, we have only mentioned a few of the numerous religions, cults and schools of thought this world has seen.

Some others are Judaism, Confucianism, Shintoism, Islam, Unity School of Christianity, Christian Science, Spiritism, Astrology, Witchcraft and Satanism, New Age and more.

You know, it is enough to boggle the mind or at least to bog one down. It should be no real source of amazement though. Man was created mind, body, and spirit. What if we were discussing religion and the spirit portion with as much certainty as we do the body portion of man's makeup? I would think someone quite foolish if he got so fed up with cookbooks, schools of dietary thought, and nutritional requirements that he flat out quit eating. Remember it is more about eating (relationship) than going to the cafeteria (church). There I go preachin' again! Oh, by the way, the very first murder recorded in human history (Genesis 4:8) was not about robbery, lust, or even in war. It had its motivation in religion!

The power of "I will" had devastating effects on mankind. The "apple clearly did not fall far from the tree" in that since the dawn of man we have each chosen sin above obedience and ran to the garment of religion rather than the innocence of relationship.

Time well spent:

Has the gene pool diminished or is man evolving still higher?

Do people have soul power?

What makes some people so dynamic?

Why are there so many religions?

Which ones are the worst?

Do you have a sin nature?

Do you believe there is such a thing a "soul ties?"

Is it possible to have an innocent relationship with God?

How?

Chapter 5

Mary had a Little Lamb: "Will I?"

*I*n the last two chapters we have discussed consequences of acts of free will. We will continue on this theme, as it is a basis for the whole book. But, there are and can be wonder-filled responses to choices that we make. It is to this end I would like to point us now.

I must confess to the reader at the outset of this discussion that I am biased. I can't explain exactly what I am about to tell you, but I will try to give a short description, and even in that I find there is a puzzlement that I don't know if I will ever find a scientific answer to—hence I have determined to take it on faith. Okay—just so you know—I am "pro-bean." Oh yeah, I love the little buggers. I find them attractive when they are growing, useful for many things we take for granted, quite tasty and frankly—a gas! See if you can wrap your brain around this mystery:

> The humble yet remarkable bean seed holds ALL the
> genetic information needed to produce a new plant

that, in turn, will produce flowers, fruit, and even new seeds to continue the whole reproductive process. Each seed is a little dormant embryo, a small, seemingly lifeless capsule, that awaits just the right conditions of water, warmth, and nutrients before it will germinate. Scientists have no trouble agreeing that the seed is alive, but in a dormant state. The tough outer layer, or testa, protects a tiny embryo inside the seed.

Warm soil and the right planting season are critical to seed germination. Once the bean seed is planted in soil warmed by the sun, the waiting embryo receives one of the critical elements it needs to grow—water. Water enters through a small hole in the seed coat called a micropyle. The micropyle not only allows water to enter the seed, but later it serves as the exit point for the radicle, the first root produced by the embryo. At this point the embryo takes its energy from two large lobes that surround it called cotelydons. The interior of the seed begins to swell as it takes in water. It continues to swell until the first root pushes its way through the hole, or micropyle, causing the seed coat and the two lobes to split apart. The first root continues its downward push, reaching gradually deeper into the soil. An amazing feature of the radicle is that it will always grow down into the soil, no matter which way it was planted. Like a slow-moving, intricate ballet, the radicle pushes downward while at the same time pushing the two lobes upward toward the surface of the soil. The part of the bean that will eventually become the stem (the hypocotyl) emerges, and continues to bend slowly and gracefully above the soil.

See *www.gardenguides.com*

I hope the above description was not too graphic. It is, of course, very scientific and truly a marvel of evolution! Right? I must also say that the above account of life beneath the surface of the soil was assuming that the planting was done in a loving and natural way? I know there are some other ways that germination can happen. . . . Forced entry for one. . . . Maybe in a lab for another. I am talking though, about a case where the gardener lovingly penetrates the soil and carefully and purposely plants the seed. I must say also that even in the case of forced entry or lab germination, it seems to me that bean-life has begun and would continue on to adulthood and purpose unless intentionally terminated. I told you I am pro-bean all the way, baby.

Seriously though, have you ever wondered how or when the first little stirring of life takes place in the process of seed growth? It seems we should wonder about that a few times since it happens zillions of times on this planet. This may seem ridiculous to many, but when faced with some of those puzzlements, I sometimes think of the scripture that says in Colossians 1:17 that all things were created by Christ and for him, and in him—**all things hold together.**

I am speculating, but before you think I am nuts, you might spend a little time studying small things. I'm talking "mad" small, the kinds of things like quarks, for example, that make cells seem huge and bean seeds like a galaxy.

I was amazed when I looked at my son's health textbook, and learned a few things they are studying about human conception.

Have you ever wondered when human life begins? It seems to me it is another one of those **boom** kinds of things. Think about it. Could somebody slowly get pregnant? I won't spend a lot of time on this but I find it interesting and so may you. If a sperm cell meets a mature egg after ovulation, it will penetrate it. "In a New York Minute" something changes in the protein coating around that egg preventing any other sperm from penetrating. I'd say that was pretty pregnant! Twenty-three chromosomes from the male seed bond or join with twenty-three chromosomes of the female egg. At the moment of fertilization the genetic makeup of that baby is determined. What color hair, eye color, some personal traits and preferences, even what size basketball shoe you will have to fork out cash for in high school—or what size crown the princess will wear at the prom! Is that cell alive then—has life begun? Or maybe when it is 8, 16, 32 . . . millions of cells? Some don't think it is alive until "it" takes its first breath! I heard recently that some say a child could be terminated even as old as two years of age. It has only then come to an age of cognition and if it was not wanted it could, and should, be killed (that isn't the term they use), all in the interest of world population control; and of course the tragedy of having a child live that was unwanted!! That is bizarre and frightening.

From time to time in our dialogue together we have taken short breaks. In the form of a time out or maybe a bunny trail. I think we need another short break. Grab a coffee and come back ready to play something similar to the famous game show, Jeopardy.

Back so soon? Okay. The category is "Classical Writers"

Player—"I'll take Classical Writers for $100"
Smartaleck—"Who wrote about 'Gallic War?'"
Player—"Julius Caesar"

Player—"I'll take Classical Writers for $200"
Smart aleck—"Who wrote the 'Annals?'"
Player—"Roman senator and historian—Tacitus"

Player—"I'll take Classical Writers for $300"
Smartaleck—"Who wrote the 'Apology?'"
Player—"Plato"

Player—"I'll take Classical Writers for $400"
Smartaleck—"Who wrote 'Nicomachean Ethics?'"
Player—"Aristotle"

Player—"I'll take Classical Writers for $500"
Smartaleck—"Who wrote the 'Illiad?'"
Player—"Homer"

Well, how did you do? I hope you remembered enough of your old history courses to at least recognize those famous names! I need to ask you something. At any time since I asked you these five questions did you find your mind doubting that these were indeed real people? Were they people of history? Or were they just mythical figures, peddled by people who were trying to conform you into their little religious box? Of course not! You accepted that these people actually lived, rose to some kind of fame and contributed to their world! (And feel free to add to the list of things you forgot in school, along with diagramming a sentence and other junk.)

It is no wonder you might recognize these famous people! The great body of evidence demands it. Let me list approximately how many surviving copies we have of each of these author's great works.

Julius Caesar. . . . . 10 copies

Tacitus . . . . 20 copies

Plato. 7 copies

Aristotle. . . . . 49 copies

Homer . . . . 643 copies

See *www.charlescarrinministries.com*

May I add just a little more sarcasm to help make my point? In the surviving works of the above authors, most, if not all of them were copied no sooner than 1,000 years after the original. Let's take just one more example of "Classical Literature", the New Testament. There are over 24,000 surviving copies of the original manuscripts. Some biblical copies are old enough to show "eyewitness" confirmation, with some copies being made within twenty-five years of the actual events. Imagine if you are over thirty years of age and you wanted to leave a description of your bedroom where you grew up, or maybe your early remembrances of childhood Christmases, so that you could pass these memories and facts down to your kids. I dare say it would be very accurate. Why is it that despite so much evidence, many people dismiss the Bible as a myth—full of errors—and man's personal interpretation? It might be similar to those who dismiss the creation evidence. Josh McDowell calls this "evidence that demands a verdict."

We are hopefully all back from our coffee break. How does any of what we have been looking at pertain to the title of this chapter? 'Mary had a little Lamb.' I want to talk about the historical figure Mary. She has also been called the mother of Jesus.

Her Hebrew name was Miriam. Mary was the wife of Joseph and the mother of Jesus Christ, who was conceived within her when she was a virgin. She is often called the "Virgin Mary," though never in scripture are those two words used together as a proper name. Little is known of her personal history. Her genealogy is given in Luke 3. She was of the tribe of Judah and of the lineage of David (Psalm 132:11, Luke 1:32). She was connected in marriage to Elizabeth who was of the lineage of Aaron (Luke 1:36). Mary's other sons included Joses (Joseph), James, Judas, and Simon. (Matthew 13:55-56, Mark 6:3).

Mary was a direct descendant of King David, which gave Jesus the right to ascend the Jewish throne, both through Mary and through adoption by his foster father, Joseph. Mary's genealogy is supplied in Luke 3:23-38. Although Jesus was clearly legally related to both parents, (to Mary by being born by her and to Joseph by being adopted by him), was he genetically related to him or his brothers or sisters?

For thousands of years, every human child has been born with an inherited sin nature and sinful flesh (Romans 8:3). This is a result of our sinful first parents, Adam and Eve, to whom we are all genetically related. Each generation (without exception) has sinned (Romans 3:23) and passed on its sinful nature and the curse of death to each succeeding generation (the biblical doctrine of imputation of sin—Romans 5:12-19). There is only one exception in history. Although Jesus grew in the womb of Mary, in the same manner as any baby, he was different from all other babies. It appears that he was not genetically related to either Mary or Joseph, for both had inherited sin nature. Jesus was sinless and one may reasonably assume, was without genetic flaw, since he was to serve as the spotless and sacrificial Lamb of God.

- Ever since Creation, each subsequent life has been created at the moment of conception. Scientifically, the new entity begins at the moment the DNA of man and woman combine. This was not the case with Jesus. As a spirit, and part of the Trinity, Jesus existed before the Creation of the world. In fact, John reveals that he is the Creator. (John 1:1)
- Furthermore, the physical body of Jesus as born in Bethlehem was clearly a special creation of God, placed in Mary's womb. This is the biblical doctrine of the Virgin Birth.

Thus, neither Christ's spirit nor his body must have resulted from the DNA of Mary's egg or from any mans sperm. Both would have contained inherited genetic defects and the sin nature. As scripture tells us, Jesus was truly the Second Adam. "The first Adam was a special creation of God, (not related to any human being), and so was the second Adam (Rom 5:12-19). Jesus was as fully human as the first Adam. And just like the first Adam, he had no sin nature, no inherited sin, and no sinful flesh, which have always been passed from one generation to the next since Adam and Eve's sin. He was absolutely pure and without sin—from the day he was born, till the day he died. He had to be—he was the Lamb of God, without blemish or spot, sacrificed for sins (John 1:29)."   See Paul S. Taylor *www.christiananswers.net*

I do hope I have helped to the establish relevance of the title of this chapter. Mary did indeed have a little Lamb. Now I want to tie this all in to the title of this book. The Power of I Will.

In the sixth month, God sent the angel Gabriel to Nazareth, a town in Galilee, to a virgin pledged to be married to a man named Joseph, a descendent of David. The angel went to her and said, "Greetings, you who are highly favored! The Lord is with you."

Mary was greatly troubled at his words and wondered what kind of greeting this might be. But the angel said to her, "Do not be afraid Mary, you have found favor with God! You will be with child and have a son, and you to give him the name Jesus. He will be great and will be called the Son of the Most High. The Lord will give him the throne of his father David, and he will reign over the house of Jacob forever; his kingdom will never end."

"How will this be," Mary asked the angel, "since I am a virgin?"

The angel answered, "The Holy Spirit will come upon you, and the power of the Most High will overshadow you. So the holy one to be born will be called the Son of God. Even Elizabeth your relative is going to have a child in her old age, and she who was said to be barren is in her sixth month. For nothing is impossible with God."

"I am the Lords servant," Mary answered. **"May it be done to me as you have said,"** *Then the angel left her.*
—Luke 1: 26-38 *(my emphasis)*

I would like to take us on the last coffee break of this chapter. In fact we will stay in coffee break mode throughout. Do you remember the catchy line comedian Joan Rivers used often? "Can we talk?" I'd like to borrow that.

Dr. Peter Stoner used to be chairman of the departments of mathematics and astronomy at Pasadena City College. He is probably best known for his work "Science Speaks", which discusses, among other things, Bible prophecies using probability estimates and calculations. Using only 8 of the 332 prophesies regarding the coming Jewish messiah, he calculated that the odds of it happening are 1 in 10 to the seventeenth power!!! And there is a 1 in 10 to the 48th power (10 with 48 more zeroes) of there being 10 prophecies coming true about this man Jesus!

I do not want to go on and on about probabilities or to wade into my thoughts on why I do not believe Mary is to be revered as an exalted being, intercessor, mediator, etc. I do want to talk about this woman Mary, a remarkable, godly, chosen vessel, and about her choices.

Have you ever thought about Mary other than as the theme of Christmas carols or nursery rhymes? I mean—here we have a young Jewish woman facing something very real. Most often in scripture, when people have an encounter with the Lord or with an angel, they fall prostrate . . . in awe . . . in fear . . . in worship. Mary seemed to survive the appearance of Gabriel quite well. I am intrigued at her response to the declaration that she will have a child. She did not say any number of things that come to mind. "You gotta be kidding me," or "I don't want a child—I have a career I need to work at first." We live in a day and age when women often choose to end the life within them simply because it is inconvenient! Sometimes because they selfishly do not want their body to bear the marks of pregnancy. Mary could have run in fear and kept this delusion to herself for years. She was not dumb in the ways of the world. She had not had sexual relations with Joseph. For that matter she had not had sexual relations with anyone. . . . "How can this be? . . . I am a virgin." I don't want to belabor—labor (or sex) here, but I wonder about these things! Jesus did not start out as a 165-pound evangelist. He started out as a divine spark fertilized embryo. And as I stated before when talking about bean seeds—nobody gets pregnant slowly!

The angel told Mary that the Holy Spirit will come upon her. Mary was not raped, nor was the Son of God conceived in a lab. The power of the Most High overshadowed her. Some people have even likened this hovering as how a lover would embrace his beloved. (Read the Song of Solomon if you think God is not the author of deep and intimate love, passion, and yes, even sex.) In a healthy, loving relationship the woman will open herself to the advances, intent, and consequences of intimacy with her mate. . . . With volition . . . by choice. Does one think for a moment that if Mary had refused the announcement by the angel, that God would have still have planted that divine seed in that chosen vessel? In the same way, I suppose, unless we open our hearts to receive the seed of new birth in Christ, he will not come into us and make his abode within us. "God with us, God in us, Emmanuel."

Does the POWER OF I WILL have any bearing in this story? I believe so. Mary answered the angel and said, "May it be done to me as you have said." That sounds to me like the long version of "I will." I believe it was at that moment—BOOM—that the consequence of her willing obedience to the power of God was set into motion. I love the Lord all the more for the beautiful story and truth that my Savior humbled himself and came to the world some centuries ago, to be born of a dear woman; that he allowed himself to be raised in a family, and that there is no phase of life or part of humanity that he did not deal with in love, empathy, and VICTORY!

Time well spent:

Do you think the Bible can be trusted historically?

How did seed germination evolve?

Do you think Mary is godlike?

Should she be worshipped?

If so, why?

If not, why?

When did Mary become pregnant?

Are humans born to live forever?

What does "God with us, God in us," mean?

Chapter 6

Upward Mobility—
the Cross:
Will you?

*U*pward mobility, strictly speaking, simply implies the capacity or facility for rising to a higher social or economic position. Another definition from the *Encarta World Dictionary* defines it as "the ability or desire to move to a higher social class and acquire greater wealth, power or status." There is nothing intrinsically wrong with any one of these goals. I said this is not a self-help book. Greater wealth, power and even status can be used for greater good!

If you study history or world religions you will find that there are many who really don't believe upward mobility is a good thing. Many communist or socialist countries say they want to help the common man or little guy, but they really promote greed and selfishness. Leaders collect goods for themselves while telling everyone else to sacrifice for the "common good." Soviet leaders had nice houses and never went without food or nice things in life while their people had to wait in line for hours for basic food, or go without basics like soap or toilet paper. Some monarchies have a ruling class that lives entirely apart from the people they govern, surrounded by wealth and opulence. Monarchies promote a strict kind of caste system where upward mobility is determined by the family you were born into. If you were born into a poor family, that was just your tough luck, your lot in life. This government-forced inequality creates a poverty mentality among the people, who naturally go into survival mode. Survival mode is exactly where that ruling mentality wants to keep the people. They are so busy with basic needs they have little time for lofty notions of self-improvement.

The average person's ability for self-improvement is severely limited or done away with completely. Without the hope of bettering one's own condition, the average person may just give up or become fatalistic. They may learn to live with their conditions and accept them, while concentrating on just providing daily needs. In a Hispanic culture you might hear the expression, "Si Dios quiere"—(if God wills it). Among Arabs you might hear the phrase, "Insha' Allah"—(God willing).

In the US, the American Dream says that anybody can become anything they desire to become and this has attracted the masses from around the world for over 200 years. And when someone comes to this country and achieves his or her dream, we applaud them. This is what our country is built upon and what our Founding Fathers intended. The Declaration of Independence laid the foundation for man's right to realize his God-given freedoms and aspirations. Our constitution has been tested, but contains the parameters to ensure these rights. We are, or certainly intended to be, a Christian nation!

Let's see what God says in his Word about prosperity and upward mobility.

If they obey and serve him, they shall spend the rest of their days in prosperity and their years in contentment
                                              —Job 36:11

He will spend his days in prosperity, and his descendents will inherit the land.
                                              —Psalm 25:13

. . . bestowing wealth on those who love me and making their treasuries full.
                                              —Proverbs 8:21

Therefore I tell you, whatever you ask for in prayer, believe you have received it, and it will be yours.
                                              —Mark 11:24

WAIT!! HOLD THE PHONE!!

Most all of what you have read so far in this chapter is to make a subtle little point. Do you see how easy it is to build a worldview? Make one statement, add a little twist to it at each point, and before long all sorts of garbage can be spewed out and sometimes forced on us. The title of this chapter was about upward mobility and the cross. We so easily let them somehow blend together. Like manifest destiny in a choir robe! I really have a problem with people who use the word of God to profit personally! I am so tired of hearing people try to position me, emotionally or intellectually, so that I will "vow a vow"—$end in a faith promi$e, $ow a $eed—to their ministry or cause. I am in no way saying we should not give to solid causes that are a vehicle to helping the needy or spreading the gospel.

> *. . . men of corrupt mind, who have been robbed of the truth*
> *and who think that godliness is a means to financial gain.*
> —1 Timothy 6:5

Do upward mobility and the cross go together? I believe upward mobility and sound biblical living *can* go together. I will admit that in my own case, it is just so stinking easy to somehow think of all the good things I would do with just a little more wealth, maybe some social status, and even a little power. I probably sound in the Lord's ears just like Tevia in Fiddler on the Roof, "Would it spoil some vast eternal plan—if I were a wealthy man?" It is just so easy for us to be misguided, and as Christians to want to get a little piece of that "American Dream", even while the masses of humanity are crying out for the Lord to return soon . . . for an end to their suffering and persecution. We want to "fund the Kingdom" while the Lord's desire is for us to **be the Kingdom.**

Before I move on, may I share with you something I found written by a Christian woman who lived from 1648 to 1717? She was imprisoned and hounded most of her life. It also shows that there is nothing really new under the sun. She contrasts the upwardly mobile "successful" Christian with those called to the inward path. This next quotation is a bit rough, but stick with me here. I think you will be glad you did.

The Less Distinct Way by Madame Guyon

Those who are led in this Way, though conducted
by a blind abandonment . . . yet experience a savory

knowledge. They never walk by the light of the intellect, like the former, who receive distinct lights to guide them, and who, having a clear view of the road, never enter those impenetrable passes of the hidden Will which are reserved for the latter. The former proceed upon the evidence furnished by their illuminations, assisted by their reason, and they do well; but the latter are destined to pursue blindly an unknown course, which, nevertheless, appears perfectly natural to them, although they seem obliged to feel their way. They go however, with more certainty than the others, who are subject to be misled in their intellectual illuminations; but these are guided by a supreme Will which conducts them howsoever it will. And further, all the more immediate operations are performed in the Centre of the Soul, that is, in the Three Powers reduced to the Unity of the Will, where they are all absorbed, insensibly following the path prescribed for them by that Touch to which we have before referred.

These latter are they who pursue the Way of Faith and absolute Abandonment. They have neither relish nor liberty for any other path; all else constrains and embarrasses them; nevertheless, there is a delicate something in the depth of the Will, which serves to nourish them, and which is, as it were, the condensed Essence of what the others experience and in ardor of purpose.

Thus they go on under the influence of this divine touch, from one degree to another, by a faith more or less sensibly savory, and experience alterations of aridity and enjoyment of the presence of God, but ever finding that the enjoyment becomes continually deeper and less perceptible, and thus more delicate and interior. They discover, too, that in the midst of their aridity, and without any distinct illumination, they are not the less enlightened; for this state is luminous in itself, though dark to the Soul that dwells in it. And so true is this, that they find themselves more acquainted with the truth; I mean that the truth is implanted in their interior, and which causes everything to yield to the Will of God. This divine Will becomes more familiar to them, and they are enabled, in their insipid way, to penetrate a thousand Mysteries that never could have been discovered by the light of reason and knowledge.

taken from *The Way to God* by Jeanne Guyon
See *www.christasus.com*

Thank you for wading through that with me. I found it interesting in that it speaks much about the Will of the Father. And it seems to point us closer to an intimate relationship rather than a religion; and yet it was written almost 400 years ago. I know "ye olde" style of thought and expression can be a bit tedious to us more highly evolved ones, who now can hardly express ourselves intelligibly and often find a need to abbreviate our text messages!

Well, what then is the cross? I dare say I would not have gotten nearly as far in the first few paragraphs of this chapter in leading you along, if I had titled the chapter "Upward Mobility and the Electric Chair." You quickly get the point. An electric chair is a means of death. The two concepts are mutually exclusive. That blessed Savior I described in the last chapter who came in the humble form of humanity, who grew with real flesh and blood, and who lived a perfect life, willfully chose to die on one of (if not the most) cruel death machines of his era.

At this point I would like to take us to the scene in the gospel of Luke where we can draw things I want us to consider about the cross. I am not going to describe the passion of Christ, the agonies, the means of torture and execution found in the cross. Those are amazing studies, but not in keeping with the theme of this book. Suffice it to say that there were three people represented in this story that were to be executed that day. The intent of the cross is much like the intent of the electric chair . . . to carry out the death sentence . . . end of story. Raised up—on a stake—either lashed or nailed—or both. Not the kind of upward mobility any of these men relished. We know that even the Lord Jesus asked the Father that this trial, this cup, be removed from him if possible—but nevertheless He chose to yield the power of His will to the WILL of the Father. Jesus knew this was part of the story he was born to fulfill.

> *So Jesus said, "When you have lifted up the Son of Man, then you will know that I am the one I claim to be, and that I do nothing on my own but speak just what the Father has taught me.*
>
> *—John 8:28*

"But I, when I am lifted up from the earth, will draw all men to myself."
He said this to show the kind of death he was going to die.
—John 12: 32,33

I wish to use one of the two men executed that day with the Lord as the central player in our talk on the power of I will. We can pick up the story told to us by the good doctor and disciple, Luke.

Two other men, both criminals, were also led out with him to be executed. When they came to the place called The Skull, there they crucified him, along with the criminals—one on his right, and the other on his left. Jesus said, "Father, forgive them, for they do not know what they are doing." And they divided up his clothes by casting lots.

The people stood watching, and the rulers even sneered at him. They said, He saved others; let him save himself if he is the Christ of God, the Chosen One."

The soldiers also came up and mocked him. They offered him wine vinegar and said, "If you are the king of the Jews, save yourself." There was a written notice above him which read: This is the King of the Jews.

One of the criminals who hung there hurled insults at him: "Aren't you the Christ? Save yourself and us!"

But the other criminal rebuked him. "Don't you fear God?" he said, "since you are under the same sentence? We are punished justly, for we are getting what we deserve. But this man has done nothing wrong."

Then he said, "Jesus, remember me when you come into your kingdom."

*Jesus answered him, **"I tell you the truth, today you will be with me in paradise."***
—Luke 23: 32-43 (my emphasis)

What kind of men were these two criminals? Sometimes they are referred to as being two sinners. Do you wonder what crime they committed? If I were to ask you whether they were good criminals or bad criminals you might just blow it off by saying something like "They were criminals . . . convicted and sentenced to die." What if I were to use the term sinners? Were they good sinners or bad sinners? What would you think? Quite likely when someone thinks of a sinner (which is really not politically correct these days), they may think of some dark and disgusting person. Bad sinners must certainly be the murderers, rapists, pedophiles, and so forth . . . right? Could they be good sinners? Maybe they were recently removed from high profile positions; maybe the kind of people that were used to having folks constantly trying to get their attention and win their favor, in the hope that they might improve their own status. Were they the upwardly-mobile movers and shakers of their day? In our time, would they have recently plundered the life savings of their trusting investors or made absurd fortunes to the detriment of others? That is not the point. It may show, however, that we have a pretty warped view of sin.

I have always liked the word picture that Chinese martyr Watchman Nee paints. He would have us look at sin more as a species than an act. If we used the examples of dogs in place of sinners, maybe that would help. We know that we can have good dogs and bad dogs. Some dogs wait eagerly for their masters to notice them, practically dislodging their tails from their spine with frantic wagging in their uncloaked happiness. They make perfect companions for little girls who would ride them like ponies . . . or an elderly person who longs for company and sometimes just a reason to live on. But the bad dog, the dirty mangy critter, the one you just can't turn your back on, the one who left lifetime scars on that little boy's face. "Put that one down, and I'll give you the gun if you don't have one of your own." I say that to show us how certain types of bad deeds can cause us to rise up in righteous indignation and demand justice. You can see the point I am trying to make here. A dog is a dog. Even the good dog could turn into the bad one in the above story, with age, with neglect, with abuse.

Jesus rocked the religious thinking of not only his day but ours. He declared that we must be born again. We need to become a different species entirely. We were born into sin. That is our nature—our spiritual and even eternal DNA—so to speak. We try so very hard to keep our identity and cling to our nature. "If we concentrate on becoming good sinners, no one will notice. After all what is sin, but an archaic notion anyway?" Besides, if we concentrate on behavior instead of the root of our condition, we can grade ourselves and others so much more easily! We say to ourselves, "I mean, I know that maybe I do _____ once in a while. But, he/she has it coming, at least I don't _____, and I would never _____!"

What does any of this have to do with the power of I will, and consequences? A lot! Not only that, but there are lessons of grace and upward mobility to be learned. Two criminals deserving death hung with the Lord that day. One mocked him. The other watched all that had preceded this execution, calculated that along with how he saw this man Jesus presenting himself during this agony, and considered what a still small voice inside him was saying. He concluded "Jesus, remember me when you come into your kingdom."

BOOM!! In a New York minute! I believe in an instant that man was born again. I believe the consequences of his "I WILL BELIEVE" ensured him of eternal life. In an instant his nature was changed and he was "saved."

"But wait a minute," you might say. "He didn't raise his hand while every eye was closed and repeat the sinners' prayer." No, he didn't do that. Nor did he receive communion, get baptized, dunked, dipped or sprinkled. He didn't join a denomination or even speak in tongues! I am sorry if I am stepping all over your theology here. Believe me, I am as apt to put God in a box as the next guy. Who doesn't like having it all figured out or pre-programmed? That way we can sort of tell who the good Christians are and who the bad ones are (even though we sometimes get bit by both!). I love true repentance and a clear cognitive salvation call, but you can't convince me that this criminal was not invited into the Kingdom of God that day, there on his cross. And I also do not believe that he was taken to a certain place in paradise where he could get the Cliff Notes on salvation, and work on it till he passed the grade! I believe it happened suddenly and I love it.

The story of the sinner whom Jesus took into paradise that day also gives me some opinions on the cross (Christianity) and upward mobility. How many people would try to rewrite that story from the Bible in modern terms? You might even hear well meaning Christians say something that hints, "If you simply come to Christ your world will radically change. You will escape the consequences (of your sexual immorality, of your stealing, of your affair), upon the lives of your children or whoever was in your sphere of influence." Sometimes, in God's grace, we have sown certain seeds and there has been a crop failure. Praise God!, because who among us has not messed up and is free from judgment? The criminal on the cross did not get a chance to come down. He could not beg for forgiveness from the parents of the child he raped, (bad sinner)—nor could he give back a portion of the life savings of those people he defrauded and live a productive life thereafter . . . *maybe making them money again,* (good sinner). He did not get a book deal. He didn't go on the evangelistic circuit or even gospel TV. Those things were said with a certain amount of sarcasm obviously, but he did not even get to go home to a loving family and lead others to the Lord or raise his children in this new Light. No sir. He died that day. The consequences he reaped were for the next and eternal life. I still love that story. It is sobering that we sometimes have to bear, and labor through, the consequences and hardships of our sinful choices; they have indeed brought death to certain aspects of our life. But it shows me that at any point in this life here . . . this time I think of as "soul school" . . . God can instantly change our destiny and even our legacy. That one who died on that cross that day still is evangelizing to this day, still pointing people toward paradise! Whodathunkit, there that day??

Time well spent:

How upwardly mobile are you, or would you like to be, on scale of 1 to 10? (10 is a real fast-tracker.)

Do you think America is a godly nation?

Is "television evangelism" the real thing?

What does the "real thing" look like?

What did you think of Madame Guyon?

Why do we like "good sinners" so much more than "bad sinners?"

In the picture preceding, which one is the one who will go home with the Lord?

Chapter 7

Self-Help (Not Really!) 501—Graduate Studies: He Will

I hope you have come along with me this far. I also hope you can see I have not tried to write the average self-help book. I call this chapter, "graduate studies," because I hope that you may have graduated to that level by now. If we are to help people come to the saving knowledge of Jesus Christ, we must do so gently. We can offer apologetics and try to give them reason to believe. Remember that nothing has been accomplished of eternal value unless they believe. We cannot earn our way into the Kingdom of God. The fact is that we can't think our way into it either. We may be totally convinced by the evidence that God exists, and in fact made the entire marvel that this world holds, and still not yield our will to his. Unless the Father draws someone providentially, he is not even able to accept the truth of God and the gospel appears as foolishness to him. It also must be said with a gulp, that even if all of the above may have been done to the letter, I may drive someone away from the King of Kings because of my lack of love and poor witness!

I have had the blessing of doing mission work in different countries for many years. The country I labored in the most by far is the island nation of Jamaica. These lovely people have been some of the most evangelized people groups in the world. Mexico had a similar influx of evangelistic teams at one point. It is not uncommon for me to be traveling back to Jamaica and see a group of people on the plane or in the airport with t-shirts on identifying themselves as a short term mission team going to or coming from Jamaica. Jamaicans themselves have a deep knowledge of scripture. They still, to this day, use the Bible in their classrooms. By this token you might expect the Jamaicans to be the most godly people on earth and the ones with the deepest enjoyment of their salvation. But that may be far from the truth. It is not uncommon for you to ask a Jamaican if they are a Christian or if they are born again and hear them say, "I used to be" or "No, I don't baptize as yet." They feel as though they may have either lost it or not earned it yet! They have a very legalistic view of salvation. Sometimes I may engage them in conversation and try to take them through the following steps. I ask them if they have ever accepted the Lord as their savior. Did they understand what they were doing and what it means for Christ to have come to earth, lived and died on the cross for the salvation of our sins? If they agree that they at one time did in fact invite the Lord into their heart, confess that they were sinners, acknowledge him as Lord and Savior, I like to ask them a question. I ask them their last name. If it is Morrison (just to make a name up) I ask them what did they do to become a Morrison? Nothing—they were born a Morrison. They can choose to be a good Morrison or a bad Morrison. They may live like a saint or live like a rum-head.

Either way they agree that they are still a Morrison. In a similar way, if they have become at one time a Christian, they may be a good Christian, (bringing pleasure to their Lord) or a bad Christian (bringing grief, grounds for discipline, and shame), but I doubt that they have lost their salvation. It is time to choose to move on to graduate studies; to move on to maturity and effectiveness and enjoyment as a child of the King.

I share all that to say this: It is my fervent prayer that you and I are born again. It is my hope that I may have written something that will have moved you toward the light and the choice of salvation if you came into this book a sinner or a skeptic. Like it or not, agree with me or not . . . you will exercise your free will in this life. You will say "I will" to one worldview or the other.

This may be the hardest chapter for me to write, because it causes me to challenge my own life. I believe all the things written so far. I have embraced the Lord, invited him to take up residence in my heart, **believed** upon him and by faith am certain of my new birth. But, if I believe all these things why do I not know a much greater sense of his presence and POWER in my life? Now that I have turned over my will to his, the remainder of my earthly life will be graduate studies, believing and receiving the rest of the HE WILL. Let's discover some of this together.

I believe you and I have tremendous power in our own will. We have free will given to us by our creator. Frankly, though, I hope I would not be too impressed if you have the iron will to become president of the lodge or even the country . . . if you can rise to stardom, fame or fortune . . . if you can even bend spoons with your will! I want to become the kind of Christian who is drawn to the saint who becomes that which the Father designed him or her to be, and who HE wills to reveal his glory through. Let me explain.

Jesus, when he was upon the earth, could have performed many fantastic feats. In fact, the devil tried his best to get the Lord to use the Power of His Will to act on his own accord with his own agenda.

> *Not everyone who says to me, "Lord, Lord" will enter the kingdom of heaven, but only he who does the* WILL *of my Father who is in heaven.*
> —Matthew 7:21

> *For I have come down from heaven not to do my will but to do the will of him who sent me.*
> —John 6:38

If that is the case, then I think we would do well to look at what the will of the Father is. It is this which gives me hope. Because if I know what his will is, I can rest in that will and plan. It was that WILL that spoke this very world into existence.

> *And this is the* WILL *of him who sent me, that I shall lose none of all that he has given me, but raise them up at the last day. For my Father's* WILL *is that everyone who looks to the Son and **believes** in him shall have eternal life, and I will raise him up at the last day.*
> —John 6:39-40 (my emphasis)

I do not have to be overly concerned with your outward performance. It is, of course, good that you and I come to maturity, that we not live as though we have not been born into a new family and kingdom (new species for that matter). But take comfort in these scriptures.

. . . for it is God who <u>works in you</u> to WILL *and to act according to his good purpose.*

—Philippians 2:13 (my emphasis)

It is God's WILL *that you should be sanctified.*

—1 Thessalonians 4:3

*Let us fix our eyes on Jesus, the **author and finisher** of our faith . . .*

—Hebrews 12:2 (my emphasis)

Now to him who is able to do immeasurably more than all we ask or imagine, according to his POWER *that is at work within us . . .*

—Ephesians 3:20

I could fill many pages with scripture verses reminding us of God's will and his power. I don't want to do that for several reasons. Sometimes evangelicals can make longs lists of quotations that they claim are God's promises to us. I think that many of them are, but I also feel that many can be taken out of context. I want to challenge us—you and me. The Lord tells us that we will do greater things than he did in the Name of the Lord, but we must remember the latter part of the verse in Matthew 7. The Lord had told his disciples on many occasions that he only did that which the Father told him to do. In John he said he only did that which he sees his Father doing. So in Matthew 7 when the Lord rebukes those who came to him saying, "Lord, Lord, did we not prophesy in your name, drive out demons, perform many miracles," let us not miss the point. These were cast out of his presence as he said he never knew them. He was not impressed with their list which, I admit, is pretty good stuff! My conclusion is that they did not do them as a result of the Father's WILL and in his POWER. The consequence for them doing something in the power of *their* will was: "I never knew you. Away from me, you evildoers."

The Lord tells us who he identifies with in Luke 8:21, "My mother and brothers are those who hear God's word and put it into practice." My challenge to you the reader and to myself is this: Let us know the Lord so intimately, that we truly become lovers; that we (like my dear wife and I) finish each other's sentences. That the power of I will becomes so overshadowed by the POWER OF THY WILL that those things more wonderful than I can ask or imagine—out of his plan and will for me—BOOM!—come to life within me, and you . . . until the will of the Father is done in this earth . . . as it is in heaven.

Selah. (pause and consider)

Please dear reader, let me know if by some work of the Spirit you may have read this conversation we've had and invited the Lord to give you that new birth. I would also love to hear reports of how the Lord may have planted a seed of his will inside of you. He is still the God of creation. He is continually unfolding new aspects of his divine plan and showing forth new works of his hand. And he does this through you and me. We are the vessels he chooses to reveal himself to all mankind. May you receive His Spirit and say, like Mary, "Be it done according to your will!"

One more note as a reminder. One day—soon maybe—we won't hear a BOOM, . . . but in the twinkling of an eye (which is faster than a New York minute) we will hear a trumpet blast. We will instantly be caught up to meet our blessed Savior and the one the saints of this world are crying out to.

~ COME SOON LORD JESUS ~

Time well spent:

Are you a little upset with God?

Is He angry or disappointed with you?

How much do you love him?

How much do you need him?

How badly does He want you?

What more will it take to get you and me to open up and say "I will?"

Are there ways to "step out of the boat" that you are not aware of?

Afraid of?

What would I rather accomplish in this life than to do the WILL *of the Father?*

Epilogue

I have just a few more comments before I feel we can say good-bye. In fact, even then, I hope it will be more of an "au revoir" than a goodbye. I have really wanted our time to be more interactive than me just talking *at* you.

I have no idea where I found you when I first said "Excuse me" in the introduction. If I were to say to you that few of us live "Norman Rockwell"-like lives, would you have any idea what I mean? It is just this. There once was a popular American artist whose paintings seemed to capture the very essence of daily life. He often painted pictures with settings of children or families that looked so innocent and carefree that you felt at ease just looking at them. One such picture had a family gathered around the table at Thanksgiving time. They had their heads bowed in prayerful thanks, hands were joined in unity, and you just knew that love and laughter were soon to follow as they enjoyed their bountiful feast.

I have lived a pretty full life and seen a lot. If I am candid with you, I might admit that there have been times when I felt I have lived a little too long and seen a little too much. As I said before, I do not know your story or where you were at the beginning of our time together. But, I would not be surprised if this book finds some of you in a life that feels anything but *Rockwell-esque* and not exactly your ideal picture of the "American Dream."

Some of you may be serving in a lonely war zone and away from children or loved ones. Some of you are behind prison bars. Some are in an abusive relationship that seems to never end. Some have a child that will not speak to you no matter how many years go by. Many have had someone pass away whose memory leaves a hole and who will forever be missed from their place at the table. Some have had a bad economy or career shifts eat away at their self-confidence, to say nothing of their savings. You know someone whose marriage is more like that of being roommates than soul mates. Some are students whose college costs keep on mounting, while prospects for work seem out of reach. Many of you live in other countries that do not celebrate our Thanksgiving and some may even hate our American Dream. But even so, all of you can still identify with a longing for love, family and wholeness.

I did not write that partial list of woes to give you indigestion after painting that picture of a Happy Thanksgiving. I did it only to come alongside of you; whether your life is *picture perfect* or more like a perfect mess! Most of us in this human condition live a life that in some way has known at least a degree of fracture, difficulty and challenge. And we certainly know others who face even harder struggles than we ourselves have.

I added this epilogue to the book to allow that we all are "works in progress." In Corinthians, the Bible likens us to living letters that are known and read by all men. What you and I do affects those in our sphere of influence as well as people we may never meet. I hope you find that the end of this book is really the beginning of a new way of approaching and experiencing life.

I have supplied thirty one pages of space at the end of this book. It cost me a little more to publish this way and for some it will remain blank. But for many of you it will be a convenient way to make the theme of this book your own. I challenge you to each day wake up and consider that this day could be the VERY day that God reveals a little more of his will for your life. I firmly believe that if you humbly and prayerfully enter this experiment with the Author of the Universe, you will not regret it. For one month (maybe 31 days) could you make notes and interact with life? Write down things that pertain to anything we have discussed. For example: world religions, human will, creation, forgiveness and grace. Is there anything that God is saying to you personally in which you could respond like Mary and say "be it done to me according to Your will?"

I wish to leave you with two of my favorite scripture verses.

Because of the Lord's great love we are not consumed, for his compassions never fail. They are new every morning; great is your faithfulness. I say to myself, "The Lord is my portion; therefore I will wait for him." The Lord is good to those whose hope is in him, to the one who seeks him; it is good to wait quietly for the salvation of the Lord.
—Lamentations 3:22-26

It is for freedom that Christ has set us free.
—Galatians 5:1

Blessings and "Au Revoir"

Day One

Day Two

Day Three

Day Four

Day Five

_____

_____

_____

_____

_____

_____

_____

_____

_____

_____

_____

_____

_____

Day Six

Day Seven

_____

_____

_____

_____

_____

_____

_____

_____

_____

_____

_____

_____

Day Eight

Day Nine

Day Ten

Day Eleven

Day Twelve

Day Thirteen

Day Fourteen

Day Fifteen

Day Sixteen

Day Seventeen

Day Eighteen

Day Nineteen

Day Twenty

_____

_____

_____

_____

_____

_____

_____

_____

_____

_____

_____

Day Twenty-One

Day Twenty-Two

Day Twenty-Three

Day Twenty-Four

Day Twenty-Five

Day Twenty-Six

Day Twenty-Seven

Day Twenty-Eight

Day Twenty-Nine

Day Thirty

Day Thirty-One

_____

_____

_____

_____

_____

_____

_____

_____

_____

_____

_____

_____

Bibliography

Flynn, Leslie, *What is Man*, Victor Books, TEC Publications, Columbus, Georgia, 1978.

Boa, Kenneth, *Cults, World Religions, and the Occult*, Colorado Springs, Colorado, Chariot Victor Publishers, 1990. *www.reflectionministries.com*.

Cottle, Ron, *Introduction to Philosophy*, Columbus, Georgia, TEC Publications, 1998.

Piper, Mel, *The Humanity of Jesus*, Broken Arrow, Oklahoma, Piper House, 1995.

Huse, Scott, *The Collapse of Evolution*, Grand Rapids, Michigan, Baker Books, 1998.

Online sites listed in text.

The author wishes to note that he remembers as a child how many Bibles contained pictures. They sometimes left as big an impression as the text and often helped generate thought. In this hope we have included several in this book.

Some proceeds from the sale of this book will be used to support our ongoing mission work with orphans and the needy in India.

Please visit www.afmindia.org.

About the Author

One place in the book we mention that everyone has what is called a worldview, "from a gravedigger to a graduate student." The author can say that he has held both of those positions. If we live long enough, and by God's blessing, we can play many roles. I have enjoyed being a son, husband and father. Other stops on the journey have included high school teacher and coach . . . business owner for over two decades . . . building contractor . . . ordained minister . . . faith based counselor . . . and missionary to several countries.

Please visit our website at *www.journey-man.org*. The author is available for speaking engagements upon request. For more information you can also contact *pilgrimceddy@yahoo.com*. We would love to hear from you. We look forward to hearing how God has led you to awesome new areas of life and His will.

Some proceeds of the sale of this book will go directly to helping the needy souls in India. Please visit *www.afmindia.org*.

Breinigsville, PA USA
24 January 2011
254006BV00002B/1/P